LANGUAGE and
LITERACY in Inquiry-Based
SCIENCE
Classrooms, Grades 3–8

LANGUAGE and LITERACY in Inquiry-Based SCIENCE
Classrooms, Grades 3–8

ZHIHUI FANG
With LINDA L. LAMME and ROSE M. PRINGLE

Foreword by Sandra K. Abell

A JOINT PUBLICATION

National Science Teachers Association

For information:

Corwin
A SAGE Company
2455 Teller Road
Thousand Oaks, California 91320
(800) 233-9936
Fax: (800) 417-2466
www.corwin.com

SAGE Ltd.
1 Oliver's Yard
55 City Road
London EC1Y 1SP
United Kingdom

SAGE India Pvt. Ltd.
B 1/I 1 Mohan Cooperative
  Industrial Area
Mathura Road, New Delhi 110 044
India

SAGE Asia-Pacific Pte. Ltd.
33 Pekin Street #02-01
Far East Square
Singapore 048763

Printed in the United States of America

Library of Congress Cataloging-in-Publication Data

Fang, Zhihui.
Language and literacy in inquiry-based science classrooms, grades 3-8 / Zhihui Fang, with Linda Lamme and Rose M. Pringle; foreword by Sandra K. Abell.
    p. cm.
Includes bibliographical references and index.
ISBN 978-1-4129-8842-1 (pbk.)

  1. Science—Study and teaching (Elementary) 2. Science—Terminology—Study and teaching (Elementary) 3. Language arts—Correlation with content subjects.
I. Lamme, Linda Leonard. II. Pringle, Rose M. III. Title.

Q181.F23 2010
372.35—dc22
                                        2010021144

This book is printed on acid-free paper.   JAN 2 4 2012

10 11 12 13 14 10 9 8 7 6 5 4 3 2 1

Acquisitions Editor:	Carol Chambers Collins
Associate Editor:	Megan Bedell
Editorial Assistant:	Sarah Bartlett
Production Editor:	Cassandra Margaret Seibel
Copy Editor:	Nancy Conger
Typesetter:	C&M Digitals (P) Ltd.
Proofreader:	Wendy Jo Dymond
Indexer:	Will Ragsdale
Cover Designer:	Scott Van Atta

Contents

Foreword   vii
  Sandra K. Abell

Acknowledgments   ix

About the Author   xi

About the Co-Authors   xiii

1. Teaching Science as Inquiry   1

    Inquiry-Based Science   2
    Language and Literacy in Inquiry-Based Science   14
    Overview of This Book   17

2. The Challenges of Science Reading   18

    What Does It Take to Comprehend a Text?   18
    Linguistic Challenges of Science Reading   22
    Conclusion   32

3. Using Trade Books to Support Science Inquiry   34

    Why Read Trade Books in Science?   35
    Award-Winning Science Trade Books   36
    Becoming Familiar With the Format
        of Science Trade Books   37
    Using Trade Books to Empower Science Learning   41
    Conclusion   48

4. Learning Language, Learning Science   49

    Building a Language-Rich Science Curriculum   51
    Developing Vocabulary Knowledge   52
    Learning About Nouns   61
    Disentangling Discourse   69
    Conclusion   75

5. Scaffolding Reading Through Strategy Instruction   **77**

Reading Strategy Instruction and Text Comprehension   78
Reading Strategy Instruction in Action: A Vignette   79
Bootstrapping Comprehension: Activating and
    Integrating Prior Knowledge   81
Monitoring Comprehension: Promoting
    Thinking During Reading   86
Consolidating Comprehension: Organizing
    Information From Text   92
Principles and Practice of Reading Strategy
    Instruction in Science   97
Conclusion   102

6. Learning to Write and Writing to Learn in Science   **103**

Why Write in Science?   103
Learning to Write Scientifically   104
Writing to Learn in Science: An Instructional Framework   111
Implementing the Writing-to-Learn-Science
    Instructional Model   113
Classroom Activities That Promote
    Writing to Learn Science   115
Conclusion   127

Endnotes   **128**

References   **134**

Index   **145**

Foreword

When my stepson, Matt, was nine years old, he was not particularly interested in reading as a leisure pursuit. He preferred to spend his free time setting traps in the back yard, endlessly hoping to capture some sort of animal. One summer, to capitalize on Matt's interest in animals, his dad helped him build an ant farm. As they puzzled over how to provide the best environment for the ants, something interesting happened. On our weekly trip to the public library, Matt, the child who never picked up a book by choice, asked, "Do you think they will have any ant books?" I seized this literacy opportunity and helped Matt find and check out every book about ants he could find. Matt "read" each book, at times skimming for the answer to a question, at times looking at photos and reading the captions, and sometimes even reading the book cover to cover. Matt had discovered how books might be useful to him. His interest in science led him to this discovery. I have known many children like Matt, turned on by the natural world but disconnected from the school-based world of reading and writing. I suspect many of you know children like Matt as well.

Matt's story illustrates that science can be the entrée into reading and writing for many of our students. However, as Zhihui Fang and his colleagues make clear in this book, being motivated to read or write about science is only one part of the picture. Even motivated young scientists can be challenged by the language and discourse style of science reading and writing. These discourse challenges can make science seem difficult and inaccessible for all but the brightest. This is certainly not the message we want to send to our students about science. We want all students to believe that they can learn science, not just the elite few.

By using the ideas in *Language and Literacy in Inquiry-Based Classrooms*, teachers can help all students build fluency with reading and writing science. The authors provide a thorough description of why science reading and writing are difficult. They also suggest a repertoire of strategies that teachers can use to help students become proficient with the language of science. Teachers who integrate these strategies into their practice increase students' opportunities to learn science; improve student motivation and self-efficacy to read, write, and do science; and increase the potential of student success, in both science and literacy.

We often think of the best science instruction as that which engages students in doing what scientists do—asking questions, collecting data, and formulating explanations from evidence. Yet reading and writing are also essential activities of scientists. As part of their professional community, scientists read the literature, write grant proposals, keep a science notebook, and present their findings. Therefore, it is not enough for the science classroom to be physically engaging. In addition to using hands-on instruction, teachers of science must engage students in reading, writing, thinking, and speaking like scientists. Knowing how and when to do so are keys to effective teaching. This book will support classroom teachers in carrying out this challenge.

Sandra K. Abell
Columbia, Missouri

Acknowledgments

We would like to thank the many preservice and inservice teachers with whom we have worked over the years. It is through them that we shared, piloted, and received feedback on many of the ideas presented in this book. We are particularly grateful to Sara Charbonnet and Melissa Henkel, two science teachers at Westwood Middle School (Alachua County, Florida), who worked closely with us in 2004 and 2005 on a reading-science integration project supported by a Multi-University Reading, Mathematics, and Science Initiative (MURMSI) grant from the U.S. Department of Education. We also thank our graduate students (Charlotte Mundy, Rebecca Norton, Mary Ellen Oslick, and Jennifer Patrick), who read draft manuscripts of this book and provided helpful comments. Finally, we acknowledge, with appreciation, our acquisitions editor Carol Collins and her team at Corwin for their guidance and professionalism throughout the publication process.

PUBLISHER'S ACKNOWLEDGMENTS

Corwin gratefully acknowledges the contributions of the following reviewers:

Sergio Z. de Alba, Teacher
R.M. Miano Elementary School
Los Banos, CA

Cynthia Ballenger, Early Childhood Specialist
Chèche Konnen Center
Cambridge, MA

Linda Keteyian, Science/Math Teacher
Priest Elementary School
Detroit, MI

Sarah J. Ramsey, Assistant Professor
The University of North Carolina at Charlotte
Charlotte, NC

About the Author

Zhihui Fang (PhD, Purdue University) is Professor of Language and Literacy Education in the School of Teaching and Learning at the University of Florida, where he also coordinates the Reading Education program. He specializes in content-area reading and writing, language development, and teacher education. His recent research focuses on the role of language in construing disciplinary knowledge and in shaping students' literacy development. He is particularly interested in exploring the use of evidence-based language and literacy practices to support science teaching and learning. Zhihui has authored over 70 publications that include books, book chapters, and journal articles. His *Reading in Secondary Content Areas: A Language-Based Pedagogy* (University of Michigan Press, 2008), coauthored with Mary Schleppegrell, describes a new approach to teaching reading in the subjects of science, mathematics, social studies, and language arts. He can be contacted at zfang@coe.ufl.edu.

About the Co-Authors

Linda L. Lamme (PhD, Syracuse University) is Professor of Education in the School of Teaching and Learning at the University of Florida, where she teaches courses in children's literature, including international literature, literature for the writing program, literature for the content areas, and multicultural literature. She conducts research on children's responses to literature, book analyses, and literature in the curriculum. Linda has served on the Notable Books for a Global Society Committee for the Children's Literature and Reading Special Interest Group of the International Reading Association, the Notable Books for Language Arts Committee for the National Council of Teachers of English, and the Children's Literature Assembly Board. She can be contacted at llamme@coe.ufl.edu.

Rose M. Pringle (PhD, Florida State University) is Associate Professor of Science Education in the School of Teaching and Learning at the University of Florida. Her areas of research include preservice teachers' positionality as science learners and issues associated with learning to teach inquiry-based science. She is particularly interested in working toward increasing the participation of minorities, especially girls of African descent, into mathematics- and science-related careers. Rose is currently exploring the relationship between science teachers' and counselors' expectations and African American girls' self-perception as science and mathematics learners. She can be contacted at rpringle@coe.ufl.edu.

1

Teaching Science as Inquiry

S cience literacy—the ability to use one's knowledge and understanding of science concepts and processes to solve realistic problems and issues for personal and social benefits[1]—has become a necessity for everyone because the society in which we live is increasingly dependent on science and technology. Despite the centrality of science to the quality of our life and to the progress of our society, many students fail to acquire even the most rudimentary science concepts, skills, and abilities. According to the 2005 National Assessment of Educational Progress (NAEP) science assessment, for example, 32% of fourth graders, 41% of eighth graders, and 46% of twelfth graders perform below the Basic level; less than one-third of the students in Grades 4 (29%), 8 (29%), and 12 (18%) perform at or above the Proficiency level; and very few students in Grades 4 (3%), 8 (3%), and 12 (2%) perform at the Advanced level.[2] International comparisons, such as the Trends in International Mathematics and Science Study (TIMSS), also indicate that the U.S. students in Grades 4 and 8 lag behind their international counterparts in some Asian and European countries in terms of both content and the set of cognitive behaviors (such as knowing, applying, reasoning) needed for successful engagement with the content.[3] A recent research synthesis by British researchers Osborne, Simon, and Collins found that students' attitudes toward science begin to decline in the upper elementary grades, and this decline accelerates rapidly after middle school (that is, from age 14 years onward).[4] Noted science educator and scholar Jay Lemke summed up the plight of science education in American schools this way:

> Too many pupils care less and less for science as a school subject the more they've taken. Too often, with the best intentions, our teaching of science frustrates students who know we expect them to understand, but who also know that they don't (even when they seem to).[5]

This disturbing state of science education has serious consequences for the preparation of a capable scientific and technological workforce, threatening to unravel the U.S. economy and undermine its global leadership. In response to the situation, the science education community has launched a series of reform initiatives aimed at improving science teaching and learning. One major reform initiative focuses on making inquiry the cornerstone of the science education curriculum.[6] Another significant strand of the recent science education reform effort is to encourage the use of language and literacy practices in support of science teaching and learning.[7] These two reform initiatives are discussed next.

INQUIRY-BASED SCIENCE

What Is Inquiry-Based Science?

During the past 15 years or so, the National Research Council and the American Association for the Advancement of Science (AAAS) have issued calls for reform in science education and published important documents to guide this reform. Among their publications, the *National Science Education Standards*[8] and *Benchmarks for Scientific Literacy*[9] are perhaps the most influential. Both documents recommended the enactment of a science curriculum that embraces an inquiry-oriented approach to science teaching. According to the National Research Council, scientific inquiry is

> a multifaceted activity that involves observation; posing questions; examining books and other sources of information to see what is already known; planning investigations; reviewing what is already known in light of experimental evidence; using tools to gather, analyze and interpret data; proposing answers, explanations and predictions; and communicating the results.[10]

Inquiry-based science recognizes science as a process of discovery and invention that involves engagement, exploration, explanation, application, and evaluation. It emphasizes developing the ability and disposition to investigate, constructing knowledge and understanding through active learning, attaining specific science process skills, and communicating scientific explanations and arguments.[11] More specifically, inquiry-based science aims to develop the following student outcomes:

> appreciating the diverse ways in which scientists conduct their work; understanding the power of observations; knowledge of and ability to ask testable questions, make hypotheses; use various forms of data to search for patterns, confirm or reject hypotheses; construct and defend a model or argument; consider alternative explanations; and gain an understanding of the tentativeness of science, including the human aspects of science, such as subjectivity and societal influences.[12]

In outlining what students should know, understand, and be able to do over the course of their K–12 education, the *National Science Education Standards* makes the point that inquiry is a step beyond the traditional process approach that focuses on lecture and demonstration. Inquiry-based science shifts the focus of science education from the accumulation of facts and the development of decontextualized science process skills to the provision of experiences that foster the development of scientific knowledge, skills, and habits of mind. It embraces the constructivist view that students learn best by doing and by active engagement. It requires students to identify assumptions, use critical and logical thinking, and consider alternative explanations.[13] Through inquiry, students learn to use scientific knowledge and processes as well as critical thinking and reasoning skills in formulating and addressing their questions. They also develop a deeper understanding of the nature of science and scientific processes as a result of their active involvement in exploring, explaining, and debating science-related phenomena and issues.

Why Inquiry-Based Science?

An inquiry-based approach shifts the focus of science teaching and learning from an interest in the accumulation of facts and concepts to the processes that engage students in actively seeking answers to their own questions or to the questions raised by others. It emphasizes the processes that scientists value for generating, validating, and renovating knowledge. As students become involved in asking questions and seeking answers, their interest in the subject will also increase. Such an engagement in the processes of science bolsters not only students' understanding of how science knowledge is constructed but also their development of scientific abilities and habits of mind.

According to the *National Science Education Standards,* a scientifically literate person is someone who

- can ask, find, or determine answers to questions derived from curiosity about everyday experiences;
- has the ability to describe, explain, and predict natural phenomena;
- is able to read with understanding articles about science in the popular press and to engage in social conversation about the validity of the conclusions;
- can identify scientific issues underlying national and local decisions and express opinions that are scientifically and technologically informed;
- is able to evaluate the quality of scientific information on the basis of its source and the methods used to generate it; and
- has the capacity to pose and evaluate arguments based on evidence and to apply conclusions from such arguments appropriately.[14]

Inquiry-based science is a powerful vehicle for developing such individuals. It promotes understanding about the nature of science, the acquisition of scientific knowledge and skills, and the cultivation of scientific habits of mind. It enables students to learn science content and use scientific understanding to make informed decisions about personal and social issues. Effective inquiry-based experiences can also help demystify some of the beliefs about science and scientists and entice more students into advanced studies in the science fields.

Several syntheses of empirical research on science teaching suggest that inquiry-based science has a positive effect on students' attitudes toward science, science achievement, cognitive development, science process skills, and understanding of science concepts.[15] For example, Wilson, Taylor, Kowalski, and Carlson designed a laboratory-based randomized control study to investigate the effectiveness of inquiry-based instruction in developing adolescent students' (aged 14–16 years) science knowledge, reasoning, and argumentation. The researchers reported that the students in the inquiry-based group reached significantly higher levels of achievement than the students experiencing commonplace, or traditional, instruction across a range of learning goals (knowledge, reasoning, and argumentation) and time frames (immediately following the instruction and four weeks later).[16] Chang and Mao compared the effects of inquiry-based instruction versus traditional teaching methods on ninth-grade students' achievement in and attitudes toward earth science. They found that the students who received inquiry-based science instruction scored significantly higher on a knowledge-based earth science content test and developed more positive attitudes toward the subject than their peers who received traditional methods of science instruction.[17] Dalton, Morocco, Tivnan, and Mead examined the effects of two approaches to hands-on science on fourth-grade students' science learning. One approach, called supported inquiry science (SIS), focused on eliciting and reworking students' misconceptions (or alternative conceptions) and coconstructing knowledge under the guidance of a teacher-coach. The other approach is called activity-based science (ABS). The researchers found that the students (with and without learning disabilities) in SIS classrooms demonstrated greater concept learning than their peers in ABS classrooms.[18]

Taken together, these studies show that an inquiry-based approach to science teaching is more effective than traditional, or commonplace, approaches in developing students' interest in and knowledge about science and in promoting their science inquiry skills and habits of mind. As Hmelo-Silver, Duncan, and Chinn concluded, "there is growing evidence from large-scale experimental and quasi-experimental studies demonstrating that inquiry-based instruction results in significant learning gains in comparison to traditional instruction and that disadvantaged students benefit most from inquiry-based instructional approaches."[19]

Translating Inquiry-Based Science Into Classroom Practice

Science teachers know the importance of inquiry, but many lack a practical framework for teaching science as inquiry to guide their instruction.[20] They face a multitude of challenges in enacting the concept of inquiry-based science in classrooms and schools.[21] These challenges include

- how to overcome technical (the meaning of inquiry), political (state mandates), contextual (school culture, resources), and personal (prior beliefs, experiences, knowledge, preference, motivation) barriers that impede the enactment of inquiry;

- how to help students formulate questions that can lead to meaningful inquiry;
- how to translate these questions into experiments and activities that extend students' conceptual understanding;
- how to guide students to make evidence-based decisions; and
- how to develop students' competence in communicating scientific findings and understanding.

As a result of these and other challenges, inquiry-based teaching remains uncommon in science classrooms.[22]

While the *National Science Education Standards* presents several vignettes of how inquiry could be enacted in the science classroom, it does not operationally define inquiry-based instruction. However, it does identify five essential features of inquiry-based science classrooms that can be used to guide instruction. These five features, along with their interpretations, are summarized below:

1. *Students are engaged by scientifically oriented questions.* These questions should be possible to investigate and aimed at probing the origins, causes, and processes related to objects, organisms, events, and relationships in the natural world.

2. *Students give priority to evidence in responding to these questions.* Students obtain accurate evidence through repeated observations and careful measurements in natural settings (like prairies or beaches) or contrived settings (like labs). They also obtain evidence from secondary sources such as teachers, textbooks, trade books, or websites. All evidence is subject to verification, questioning, and further investigation.

3. *Students formulate explanations from evidence.* Explanations are based on logic and reasoning, instead of personal beliefs, religious values, myths, or superstition.

4. *Students evaluate their explanations in light of alternative explanations.* Students learn about other possible explanations through sharing with peers and reading related materials. This process should lead students to refine or reconsider their own explanations based on the available evidence.

5. *Students communicate and justify their explanations.* Students demonstrate the ability to articulate their questions and hypotheses, describe investigative procedures and the experimental evidence, present plausible explanations, and develop logical arguments based on an examination of existing scientific knowledge.[23]

Sample strategies for incorporating these features into the science classroom are presented in Table 1.1.

Table 1.1	Strategies for Incorporating Essential Features of Inquiry Into Science Classrooms

Essential Features of Inquiry	Teaching Activities
Engaged by scientifically oriented questions	• Provide opportunities for students to observe and explore their surroundings, which should lead them to generate questions about the natural world. • Have students read relevant texts and use the reading as a springboard to get students to raise and discuss relevant issues and questions. • Guide students to reframe or reword their questions or wonderings into forms that can be investigated. • Work with students to turn the purposes or objectives of traditional science activities into research questions.
Give priority to evidence	• Give students opportunities to identify variables, develop procedures, and devise strategies for collecting and presenting data. • Engage students in data analysis through a search for patterns and themes.
Formulate explanations from evidence	• Encourage students to construct explanations based on the experimental evidence. • Discuss with students that explanations based on personal beliefs or religious values may be interesting, but are not scientific.
Evaluate explanations	• Introduce information from the text and engage students in comparing and contrasting their own explanations with those provided in the text or offered by their peers.
Communicate and justify proposed explanations	• Encourage students to talk with their peers about their inquiry. • Provide opportunities for sharing through written and oral presentations. • Involve students in debates. • Allow students to challenge their own explanations and those of their peers.

The implementation of the five essential features of inquiry does not have to proceed in a linear fashion. Depending on the goals of the curriculum and the students' level of cognitive development, teachers can vary the ways in which these essential features are included and developed in the classroom; they can also adjust the level of inquiry during instruction. For example, teachers can choose to focus on developing students' abilities to formulate scientifically oriented questions in a particular science activity. If, however, the focus of the activity is on formulating explanations from evidence, teachers can guide students in collecting data, analyzing data, and generating explanations based on the experimental evidence. In some cases, students may need to develop the skills of observation and measurement and be able to manipulate experimental instruments before they can effectively collect and record data. Understanding variables and principles of "fair testing" (that is, making sure only one factor, or variable, is changed at a time while keeping all other conditions the same) is also important and should be considered when planning for inquiry-based science. Above all, classroom investigations should be guided by concepts, performed not only to verify rules but also to test ideas, and aimed at developing students' skills to think logically and critically about the relationships among evidence, claims, warrants, and explanations.[24]

Teaching science as inquiry places new demands on teachers. It requires them to go beyond their traditional role as knowledge transmitters to forge collaborative partnership with their students. Barbara Crawford proposed a model of inquiry teaching that embraces the following six characteristics: contextualize instruction in authentic problems, focus on grappling with data, forge collaboration between teacher and student, make connections with society, model behaviors of scientists, and develop student ownership.[25] This model embraces inquiry as both content and pedagogy and calls for active and complex teacher participation. It requires teachers not only to serve as knowledge facilitators or guides, but more importantly to engage students in the kinds of cognitive processes and behaviors used by practicing scientists. This means that the level of teacher involvement in inquiry-based classrooms is significantly greater than in traditional classrooms.

In teaching science as inquiry, teachers can vary the level of inquiry—and thus the amount of support they provide to students—on a continuum from a more structured, teacher-controlled format to more open-ended explorations initiated by students. Because it takes time for students to develop the confidence and skills needed for doing inquiry, teachers need an incremental approach when transitioning to a more extensive inquiry-based science curriculum. Ideally, teachers should tailor inquiry lessons to the readiness and developmental levels of their students. They can gradually increase the level of inquiry by moving along the following continuum:

- *Level 0 (No Inquiry):* Provide the problem, procedures, and methods to students and have them conduct an experiment to confirm a principle in which the results are known in advance.
- *Level 1 (Low Level of Inquiry):* Have students investigate a problem presented by the teacher using procedures and methods provided by the teacher. Students interpret the data and propose viable solutions to the problem.
- *Level 2 (Moderate Level of Inquiry):* Have students investigate a problem presented by the teacher using procedures and methods they choose or develop. Students decide what data to collect, how to interpret the data, and what explanations or solutions to propose for the problem.
- *Level 3 (High Level of Inquiry):* Have students investigate a problem they generated from a "raw" phenomenon using procedures and methods they choose or develop. They decide what data to collect, how to interpret the data, and what explanations or solutions to propose for the problem.[26]

Understanding that inquiry can be implemented with increasing student responsibilities allows teachers to offer the appropriate scaffolds needed to develop target knowledge, skills, and habits of mind.

Sample Inquiry-Based Science Lessons

To illustrate the principles of inquiry-based science, we provide two sample lessons (see Figure 1.1 and Figure 1.2) in which students were engaged in both hands-on (firsthand) and minds-on (secondhand) tasks of inquiry.

The inquiry-based approach as depicted in Mrs. Kaplan's and Mr. Bellamy's lessons reflects what has recently been recommended by the science education community and is believed to be most effective in developing students' scientific literacy. Like scientists who develop their knowledge and understanding as they seek answers to questions about the natural world, the students in both classrooms actively and collaboratively engaged in the "sciencing cycle" of recognizing a problem; formulating an investigatable question; proposing

Figure 1.1	An Inquiry-Based Science Lesson on Rocks

Exploring Rocks

The fourth graders in Mrs. Kaplan's class were seated in a circle on the floor for the usual morning meeting. It was the first day after spring break, and Mrs. Kaplan's plan was to have each student share an interesting event from his or her experience during the previous week. Payton was the second student to share. He pulled a plastic baggie from his backpack and placed it on the floor. "I went to a beach in California and I collected these rocks," he said. The teacher had Payton pass the collection around and everybody in the class took a rock to look at more carefully. "Wow! Mine has different colors," Madison screamed. "Mine too," echoed Jayda, who liked to write poems about rocks. "Look at the shape of this one," Diego said. Mrs. Kaplan was so excited about what the children had to say about rocks that she allowed an extra five minutes for them to share their observations. She knew that her lessons on minerals and rocks before the break had rubbed off on the children.

As the children continued to talk amongst themselves about rocks, Mrs. Kaplan drew three columns on the board and labeled them K (what I Know), W (what I Want to know), and L (what I have Learned). (This is called a K-W-L chart.) She instructed the children to go back to their seats and think about some things they already knew about rocks. After a few minutes, she asked, "Ok, so what do we know about rocks?" The children shouted a barrage of responses, including "They are hard," "There are different types," "Small rocks come from bigger ones," and "Rocks can make dirt." The teacher wrote these responses on the board, in the column labeled K.

"What questions do you have about rocks?" Mrs. Kaplan asked next. As the children responded, she recorded their questions on the board in the second column, labeled W. Some of the questions she recorded were "How are rocks made?" "Where do rocks come from?" and "How many different types of rocks are there?"

Mrs. Kaplan then divided the class into teams of four and gave each team a hand lens and a box of rocks she had procured in preparation for the science unit. She wrote the word *classify* on the board and held a discussion about what the word means. When she was sure that the children understood that *classify* means organizing things into groups based on similarities and differences, the teacher instructed the class to begin observing the rock collection in their box. She reminded the class of the procedures for appropriate use of a hand lens in making observations and then underlined the question "How many different types of rocks are there?" on the board. She asked the children to note in their science journals the colors and textures of their rocks, whether there were grains or crystals in the rocks, and what clues they could see that indicated how the rocks were formed. The children were to organize their rocks into groups and write down the features they used in separating them.

After fifteen minutes, Mrs. Kaplan had each team share what they did with their rocks. Four of the six teams classified their rock collections into three groups. The other two teams reported that they had classified their rocks into four groups. Mrs. Kaplan conducted a whole-class discussion, asking the children what features they used to classify the rocks. As each feature was identified, she strategically wrote it on one of the three chart papers she had previously taped to the wall. She then distributed a set of six books to each of the four teams that had organized the rocks into three groups, instructing them to pick a book to read and find the answer to the question "What are the three types of rocks?" She reminded students to use the table of contents or index in the books to look for the information they needed. The six books that Mrs. Kaplan handed out were *Rocks* by Alice Flanagan[27], *Rocks and Minerals* by Ruth Chasek[28], *A Look at Rocks* by Jo S. Kittinger[29], *Rocks and Minerals* by R. F. Symes[30], *Rocks Tell Stories* by Sidney Horenstein[31], and *Rocks and Minerals* by Herbert S. Zim and Paul R. Shaffer[32]. These books had been purposefully chosen to accommodate different reading levels among the students.

Mrs. Kaplan then went to the other two teams and guided the children in making further observations of the rocks. Soon, a consensus was reached among the members of the two teams that their rocks should have been separated into three groups, at which time the teacher handed each team the same set of six books and instructed them to read and respond to the same question (that is, What are the three types of rocks?).

There was a buzz in the room as the children began to figure out the three types of rocks. They were now eager to say and write the names on the chart paper on which the features were written. Three children were allowed to write the words, *Igneous, sedimentary,* and *metamorphic* on the respective chart paper corresponding to the features. Mrs. Kaplan then challenged the class to classify the piece of rock they were given from Payton's collection and explain the reasons for their decisions.

As a homework assignment for the week, Mrs. Kaplan asked the children to pick two or three books to read at home from the trade book collection on rocks and minerals that she had checked out from the school and county libraries. All students were required to bring the notes they took during reading to help their teams compose a report about rocks for inclusion in the class newsletter that was to be shared with the second graders in the school. To help her students take good notes during reading, Mrs. Kaplan had planned to conduct a lesson on two-column note taking (see Chapter 6) the next day.

A sample rock report, composed by Payton's team, follows.

Rocks have been around for thousands of years. They can be found almost anywhere. There are three kinds of rocks: igneous, sedimentary, and metamorphic.

Igneous rocks are formed by magma. Magma explodes out of a volcano and then hardens up. If it hardens quickly, it will have large crystals. If it hardens slowly, it will have small crystals or no crystals. It will look glassy. Some igneous rocks are obsidian and basalt.

Sedimentary rocks are formed when sediment, sand, soil, and gravel pack together. Fossils are sometimes found in a sedimentary rock. Some sedimentary rocks are granite and limestone.

Metamorphic rocks form when a sedimentary rock, igneous rock, or another metamorphic rock sinks to the core of the Earth and it changes by heat and pressure. Crystals are very common in these rocks. Fossils are sometimes found too. Some metamorphic rocks include gneiss, which comes from granite, and marble, which comes from limestone.

These are the three basic kinds of rocks on Earth.

Figure 1.2   An Inquiry-Based Science Lesson on Acids and Bases

Investigating Acids and Bases

It's Tuesday afternoon in Mr. Bellamy's seventh-grade science classroom, where students were learning about acids and bases. The lesson began with the teacher reviewing the textbook excerpts the class had been reading over the last week. The excerpts were about acid rain and its impact on limestone topography. The review ended with the students raising questions about the chemical nature of other substances such as water, soda, and vinegar and how these substances react with limestone. The questions were written on a piece of chart paper. Through class negotiations, the students decided to explore the acidity and alkalinity of a range of everyday substances.

Mr. Bellamy divided the class into groups of four and gave each group a few substances, such as tap water, distilled water, vinegar, and popular soda drinks (like Pepsi, Coke, Sprite). He then wrote the following questions on the Smart Board: (a) What is the pH of each of these substances? and (b) How is the pH of each substance related to acidity and alkalinity? The students discussed these two questions in their groups, generating hypotheses and brainstorming ideas for testing them. Mr. Bellamy listened in on the conversations, encouraging each group to decide how to proceed toward answering the two questions.

As the students began to conduct their experiments, Mr. Bellamy went from one group to the next, making observations and asking questions. His goal was to ensure that his students worked like scientists—discussing ideas among themselves, documenting their observations, and using data to verify predictions and draw conclusions. He noticed that each group was proceeding at a different pace. One group in the front of the room, for example, was deciding on how best to represent their data. The group members all agreed on using a table but were struggling with an appropriate title for each column in the table. Other groups had begun testing the substances with the universal indicator.

When he moved to the last group of four girls in the back of the room, Mr. Bellamy noticed that they had already tested their substances and recorded the data in a table. The group was using the evidence to arrive at a conclusion. When the girls declared that they were finished, Mr. Bellamy prompted them to compare their conclusion about acids and bases with the information presented in their science textbook. "Now, everyone," he said, "let's reread the section on acids and bases in the textbook and see if the conclusions you have drawn from your experiment are supported in the text. You should also consider reading one of the three books in our classroom library to determine what other activities you might conduct to extend your knowledge about acids and bases." The three books that Mr. Bellamy referred to were *Acids and Bases* by Rebecca Johnson,[33] *Acids and Bases* by Carol Baldwin,[34] and *Acids and Bases* by Chris Oxlade.[35] He had bought them for use with the unit.

When all groups concluded their experiments, Mr. Bellamy held a class discussion to address the two questions he had posed earlier about the pH values of everyday substances and their relationship to acidity and alkalinity. Toward the end of the discussion, Mr. Bellamy prepared his students for next week's topic on "acids in the atmosphere" by asking them to read related trade books in the classroom and school libraries and gather information about the topic on the Internet. The students were to prepare a letter to a local newspaper discussing the impact of acids on the environment and what the government had done to regulate acid emissions from a local chemical plant. To prepare his students for the writing task, Mr. Bellamy had planned a lesson on paraphrasing (see Chapter 4), a strategy for translating the technical, dense language of science texts into a more commonsense type of language that is comprehensible to the newspaper readership.

hypotheses; designing and conducting an experiment; using appropriate tools and techniques to collect, analyze, and interpret data; developing descriptions, explanations, predictions, and models based on evidence; drawing conclusions; communicating results and arguments; and generating additional questions for further inquiries. Both teachers emphasized the development of science knowledge, skills, habits of mind, values, and attitudes by providing opportunities for their students to ask questions, explain problems, design and carry out experiments, engage in reading and writing, interpret information, share ideas, validate conclusions, and communicate understandings.

In Mrs. Kaplan's lesson, the fourth graders developed their conceptual understanding of rocks through not only the firsthand experience of examining real rocks but also the secondhand experience of reading books about rocks and discussing and writing about rocks. The K-W-L chart was used to activate the students' prior knowledge and help them set a purpose for inquiry. During the hands-on experience, the students engaged in collecting data and using the data to make grouping decisions for their rock collections. The home reading assignment allowed the students to gain more in-depth information about rocks, furthering their inquiry into and learning about the topic. The two-column note-taking lesson prepares the students for the writing project. The publication of a class newsletter promotes the use of language to communicate what the students have learned and understood about rocks.

In Mr. Bellamy's lesson, the seventh graders raised a number of questions based on their reading of the science textbook and the ensuing class discussion. One of the questions became the focus of class inquiry. The teacher then provided experiences that fostered deep and robust conceptual understanding by encouraging his students to design experiments, make predictions, collect data, propose explanations, consider alternative explanations, and draw conclusions. He also encouraged his students to connect science with society by having them write a letter to the editor of a local newspaper discussing the environmental impact of acids. The lesson on paraphrasing prepares the students to make appropriate use of language according to the purpose and audience of the writing task.

The approaches used in Mrs. Kaplan's and Mr. Bellamy's classes are different from how science has traditionally been taught. In most classrooms, teachers are viewed as experts who provide carefully outlined procedures for the completion of assigned science activities. Usually these activities lead to one "correct" answer, often believed to be located in the textbook. What is required is the development of specialized skills, such as the ability to follow instructions and manage activities within a given timeframe. In many instances, these skills are developed out of context and are unrelated to the activities that investigate and analyze science questions. In short, traditional science teaching reinforces the myth of science as a body of information or facts created by experts for students to memorize. The inquiry-based approach illustrated in the two sample lessons, on the contrary, portrays science as a process for understanding the natural world and as a way of thinking and reasoning. It also allows for the use of diverse methods to develop and renovate knowledge in science.

LANGUAGE AND LITERACY IN INQUIRY-BASED SCIENCE

In Mrs. Kaplan's and Mr. Bellamy's lessons, reading and writing are an integral part of inquiry, as students use texts (textbooks, trade books, websites, and so on) to generate questions, access information, validate conclusions, communicate knowledge and understanding, and stimulate further inquiry. The two lessons exemplify a second strand of the current science education reform, which is to encourage interaction between the literacy and the science education communities.[36] This reform initiative recognizes that science is a process of inquiry conducted through the use of language. On one hand, science is an organized human activity that seeks knowledge about the natural world in a systematic way. It requires the use of scientific methods for observing, identifying, describing, and experimentally investigating the natural phenomenon. On the other hand, science is also a form of discourse involving the use of language, particularly written language. Scientists use language in conducting scientific inquiries and in constructing theoretical explanations about the natural phenomenon. They also use language to communicate scientific knowledge, principles, procedures, and arguments to others. This means that to be truly literate in science, students must be able to both conduct scientific inquiries and read and write science texts. Canadian science educators Stephen Norris and Linda Phillips captured this duality of science literacy by indicating that students need not only to be knowledgeable about the substantive content of science (that is, the derived sense of science literacy) but also fluent in the language and discourse patterns of science (that is, the fundamental sense of science literacy).[37]

This renewed emphasis on the role of language and literacy within science education is warranted on several grounds. First, language was and still is the principal resource for making meaning in science.[38] It enables scientists to construct, organize, communicate, interpret, and challenge scientific knowledge, claims, and arguments. According to Norris and Phillips, the development of modern Western science is dependent on written language and reading and writing are "inextricably linked to the very nature and fabric of science."[39] This means that the ability to read and write science texts is no longer an optional extra in

> The ability to read and write science texts is no longer an optional extra in science education.

science education. It is, in the words of British science educators Jerry Wellington and Jonathan Osborne, "an absolute essential for the development of scientific literacy."[40] Without the ability to read and write science texts, students are severely handicapped in their inquiry endeavor and limited in the depth and breadth of scientific knowledge and skills they can attain.

Second, reading and writing are powerful vehicles for engaging students' minds, for fostering the construction of conceptual understanding, and for supporting inquiry and problem solving in science.[41] Reading and writing involve many of the same cognitive skills and processes that are central to inquiry science, including predicting, inferring, monitoring, making connections, analyzing, verifying, drawing conclusions, problem solving, interpreting, and critiquing. They provide an opportunity for students to engage in secondhand investigations that reinforce, extend, and enhance the firsthand experience of experiments and observations.[42]

Third, reading and writing constitute an integral part of the social practices that scientists engage in. Real scientists read and write articles in their fields with care and critical-mindedness.[43] They read to evaluate the information and arguments presented in the text and make judgments about the trustworthiness of knowledge claims. They also write to reflect on their thoughts and ideas, to offer alternative explanations of the science phenomenon or issue at hand, and to document proprietorship of intellectual properties.[44]

Fourth, it has been demonstrated that school science texts are simultaneously dense, technical, abstract, and complex.[45] These texts are different from the more familiar and "friendly" storybook texts that students are used to reading and writing in the primary years of schooling (Grades K–2). Students need new language skills and literacy strategies to handle the more demanding reading materials that are required of them beyond the primary grades. However, many preadolescents and adolescents lack such skills and strategies. They often have misconceptions about science reading, science text, and science reading strategies.[46] Recent evidence suggests that a staggering number of students in Grades 4 through 8 are not able to read and comprehend content-area texts in school subjects such as science. According to the 2005 NAEP reading assessment, for example, 38% of fourth graders and 29% of eighth graders are reading below the Basic level, meaning that they are not able to demonstrate an overall understanding of what they read; less than one-third of fourth and eighth graders read at or above the Proficiency level, a level that is considered essential for academic success.[47] This situation necessitates a continuing emphasis on language and literacy beyond the primary grades so as to ensure that students develop new skills and strategies for successfully interacting with content-area texts.

> *A staggering number of students in Grades 4 through 8 are not able to read and comprehend content area texts.*

Fifth, empirical research has provided substantial evidence that suggests integrating language and literacy practices with science can significantly improve students' engagement with and learning of science.[48] These studies demonstrated that by providing students time to read and write science and by teaching them how to use a repertoire of reading and writing strategies, teachers could not only enhance students' capacity to comprehend and compose science texts (that is, the fundamental sense of science literacy) but also their science knowledge, habits of mind, and inquiry skills (the derived sense of science literacy).

In short, the current push to make language and literacy a legitimate part of science education has both theoretical and empirical support. It has heightened the awareness within the science education community of the role language and literacy plays in informing science teaching and in empowering science learning. Increasingly, there are calls for science teachers to embed language and literacy practices in authentic science inquiry "so that all students have a greater chance of fully achieving science literacy."[49]

OVERVIEW OF THIS BOOK

This book responds to the recent call for science teachers to use documented language and literacy practices in support of science teaching and learning. It describes ways to integrate language analysis, reading and writing strategy instruction, and quality trade books into inquiry-based science classrooms, helping science teachers more effectively promote science literacy development for all students.

The book is intended for science teachers in Grades 3 through 8. It is also suitable for reading teachers, literacy coaches, and those who are interested in infusing language and literacy practices into content-area instruction. The book can be used in professional development workshops, institutes, and study groups. It is also appropriate for science methods and reading methods courses, as well as for topical seminars in science or literacy education.

The book consists of six chapters. Chapter 1 (this chapter) discusses and illustrates the notion of inquiry-based science as defined by the science education community and presents a rationale for integrating language and literacy practices into the science curriculum. Chapter 2 discusses what it takes to comprehend a text and identifies the key grammatical features of science texts and the challenges these features present to reading comprehension. Chapter 3 explains the rationale for infusing trade books in the science curriculum, describes key resources for finding quality science trade books, identifies several additional skills needed in reading science trade books (beyond those discussed in Chapter 2), and describes the many ways trade books can be used to empower science learning. Chapter 4 presents a variety of discipline-specific language-based strategies for helping students cope with the often technical, dense, abstract, and complex texts of science. Chapter 5 describes the "what" and "how" of nine reading strategies for scaffolding students' interaction with science texts before, during, and after reading. Chapter 6 presents information on how to help students learn to write basic school-based science genres and to use writing as a tool for learning science. Taken together, the entire volume provides a wealth of evidence-based strategies, practical ideas, and valuable resources for infusing language and literacy practices into inquiry-based science classrooms.

2

The Challenges
of Science Reading

We saw in Chapter 1 that Mrs. Kaplan and Mr. Bellamy use language and literacy to support inquiry-based science in their classrooms. Because language and literacy are a legitimate part of science, Wellington and Osborne have suggested that students "need to be trained in the art of reading science—and to be given practice in it."[1] Many teachers, however, believe that by the end of second grade, students have learned how to read and, by extension, mastered the skills and strategies necessary to comprehend and learn from content area texts in later years of schooling. This is not the case. We suggest in this chapter that there is a need to continue to support students' language and literacy development beyond the primary grades (K–2) because the challenges that students face in reading the specialist texts of the curriculum content areas in intermediate grades (3–8) and beyond are in many ways different from those they experience in reading the more everyday texts of earlier grades.

WHAT DOES IT TAKE TO COMPREHEND A TEXT?

There is little doubt that the main goal of reading should be comprehension. But what does it take to comprehend a text? How is reading in the primary grades different from reading in the intermediate grades?

Answers to these questions will help teachers better understand what constitutes sound instructional practices in science reading for Grades 3 through 8. In this chapter, we take a close look at the processes underlying the comprehension of two texts—a primary grade story and an intermediate-grade science explanation (see Table 2.1)—and draw implications of this examination for reading instruction in science. The storybook text is an excerpt from "Arthur's TV Trouble," which is included in the popular children's series *The World of Arthur and Friends*[2] and represents the type of text that constitutes the main literacy staples for primary-grade children. The expository excerpt, on the other hand, is about photosynthesis in plants and is more typical of the sort of texts that intermediate-grade students are likely to encounter in their reading. It comes from the plants issue of *Kids Discover*[3], an award-winning magazine widely regarded as most suitable for children ages eight to twelve.

Table 2.1   Arthur Text and Plant Text

Arthur Text	Plant Text
"Arthur's TV Trouble"	**"Reaching for the Light"**
Ads for the Treat Timer were everywhere. Now Arthur really wanted one.	Light is so important to the survival of plants that they seem to reach toward it. But how does a plant 'know' which way to grow? A plant may not have eyes to tell it where the light is, but a plant does have hormones. Hormones are substances produced by plants (and animals) that regulate growth and development. Auxins are hormones that affect the growth of plant cells. Auxins cause cells on the shady side of a plant to grow faster than cells on the sunny side. As a result, a plant's stem may bend toward the light to allow as much light as possible to reach the maximum number of food-making cells. This phenomenon is known as phototropism.
Arthur counted his money. D.W. helped.	
"Even with all of my birthday money," he said, "I only have ten dollars and three cents."	
"I know what you're thinking," said D.W. She ran to protect her cash register.	
Arthur decided to ask Dad for an advance on his allowance	
"Gee, I'd love to help," said Dad, "but my catering business is a little slow right now."	
Arthur knew Mom would understand.	
"Money doesn't grow on trees," said Mother, "and I think Pal likes treats from you, not a machine."	

Comprehending the Arthur Text

In order to comprehend the Arthur text, readers must be able to recognize at least 90% of the words in the excerpt and understand what they mean. Readers must also be able to read the text with some degree of fluency using appropriate speed, phrasing, prosody, and intonation so that they can channel enough cognitive resources to build a "situation model"[4] that the text projects. Building such a situation model, however, requires not just knowledge of individual words and sentences, which are in this case remarkably similar to those that children typically use in their everyday social interaction with peers and family members. Readers need, in addition, a "cultural model" of a Western, middle-class childhood and relevant personal experiences. According to American sociolinguist James Gee,[5] a cultural model is one's everyday theories—storylines, images, schemas, metaphors, and models—about a particular cultural phenomenon, such as a birthday, Halloween, or Mardi Gras.

For example, readers will need to have a concept of the advertisement-oriented capitalist economy and understand the role of TV, radio, and newspaper commercials in enticing children (and adults) into purchasing merchandise that may otherwise be unknown to the public. In addition, readers will need to know other commonsense concepts, such as

- birthday money—the significance of and the rituals associated with birthdays in American children's lives;
- cash register—the concept of a piggy bank for children in American middle-class families; and
- advance on allowance—allocation of financial resources in American middle-class families.

Based on an understanding of these and other concepts, readers must also be able to make the following inferences:

- "Catering business is slow" means Dad is not earning enough income for the family and thus cannot afford to give Arthur spending money. This also assumes that children's toy machines are not essential to the livelihood of the family.
- "Money doesn't grow on trees" means that money is not easy to come by, and therefore, Mom cannot allow Arthur the luxury of spending money on toys.
- "Arthur counted his money" presumes that Arthur has his own savings at home. This is possibly related to the "allowance"

concept earlier, suggesting that Arthur's money might have come, at least in part, from his allowance. Readers must be able to bridge conceptual gaps like this one in order to make intra-textual connections.

- The Treat Timer must cost more than 10 dollars and 3 cents or be significantly more than the amount that Arthur would like to take out of his existing savings.
- "D.W. ran to protect her cash register" implies that D.W. also has a piggy bank of her own. She probably has her own allowance as well.

In addition, readers must be able, based on their cultural models of Western middle-class childhood and on their knowledge of the other books in the Arthur series, to infer the relationship between Arthur and D.W., determine what the Treat Timer might be, guess who Pal is, and make a connection between the Treat Timer and Pal.

It is obvious from this analysis that reading is indeed a complex task that involves the orchestration of a multitude of processes. These processes cannot be set in motion without the following three things:

- Understanding the language (words, sentences, discourse structure) through which the story is constructed
- Possession of relevant experiences and background knowledge that are stated, assumed, implied, or taken for granted in the text
- Command of a repertoire of reading strategies that promote the activation and use of cognitive and metacognitive skills (predicting, monitoring, inferencing, visualizing, questioning) to regulate the reading processes

Comprehending the Plant Text

Now let's look at the science (plant) excerpt and see what it takes to comprehend it. As is the case with the Arthur excerpt, linguistic knowledge, relevant background knowledge, and reading strategies are all needed in order for comprehension of the plant text to occur. While the reading strategies (such as activating background knowledge, doing think-alouds) needed for engendering the use of cognitive and metacognitive skills apply to both texts, the linguistic and background knowledge required for the plant text differs considerably from that required for the Arthur text. With the Arthur text, the background knowledge that is needed is what we would call mundane, or commonsense, knowledge; it is acquired largely through everyday social interaction with family members, friends, and others with shared experiences. On the other hand, the background knowledge required for the plant text is further removed from children's everyday ordinary life. It is more specialized and not likely to be picked up from everyday informal social interactions with friends and family members. It is, instead, typically acquired through schooling and a wide reading of related materials.

In terms of language, the Arthur text sounds familiar and comfortable because its language closely approximates the type of language that children normally use in their everyday social lives. Children can understand it with relative ease when the text is read silently or aloud to them. On the contrary, the language that is used to construct the specialized knowledge about plants sounds much less like speech. It is less familiar, less comfortable, and more alienating than the storybook language. It is, in short, more challenging for children to comprehend. What exactly are the sources of this comprehension difficulty? This is the subject of our discussion in the rest of this chapter.

Each of the three pillars of text comprehension—linguistic knowledge, background (including content) knowledge, and reading strategies—is taken up in this book. In the rest of this chapter, we address the issue of linguistic knowledge by discussing the key grammatical features of science texts, the functions of these features in scientific meaning making, and the comprehension challenges these features present for children.

LINGUISTIC CHALLENGES OF SCIENCE READING

As students move through school science from elementary to middle and high schools, they also take a linguistic journey through the history of science.[6] In primary-grade science, students typically engage in activities that aim at replicating past scientific discoveries through observations of easily observable phenomenon and experimentation with simple hands-on tasks. The genres needed to describe and explain these activities (procedures, instructions, recounts) have been established in science for some time. The language used in these genres is similar to the kind of language that children use in daily social interactions. However, the science of later years of schooling tends to be more advanced, focusing on more recent scientific knowledge and discoveries. The language needed for construing the more advanced science is more specialized, with genres such as reports, explanations, and expositions constructed in complex grammatical patterns. We describe several key features of this language below, drawing examples from the plant text as well as other reading materials in school science.

Technicality

As noted earlier, the plant text deals with a topic—photosynthesis—that is far removed from children's everyday life. In other words, the text is more technical and specialized than the Arthur text. The technicality of the plant text is constructed with two types of words—those that are specifically coined for and unique to the field of science and those that occur regularly in children's everyday speech but assume nonvernacular meanings when used in the science context. Words such as *hormones, auxins, cells,* and *phototropism* belong to the first category. Words that belong to the second category include *know, substances, stem,* and *regulate.* Together, these two types of words convey specialized meanings that explain the concept of photosynthesis.

Comprehension problems can arise when there is a heavy concentration of technical words in a short chunk of text, as the following excerpt from a seventh-grade science textbook exemplifies:

> When an **impulse** reaches the end of an **axon**, a **chemical** is **released** by the **axon**. This **chemical diffuses** across the **synapse** and starts an **impulse** in the **dendrite** or **cell body** of the next **neuron**.[7]

With technical vocabulary (in bold) constituting roughly one-third of the total words, this excerpt can present significant problems for both decoding and comprehension. Students need to develop strategies for learning technical vocabulary in science texts.

Abstraction

The plant text is also more abstract than the Arthur text. What makes the plant text more abstract is the use of not only technical vocabulary but also certain nouns, such as *survival, growth, development,* and *phenomenon.* Nouns like these derive from—and are normally expressed in the more concrete language of everyday life as—verbs. The correspondence between these nouns and their verb counterparts is shown below:

Verb	Noun
survive	→ survival
grow	→ growth
develop	→ development
happen/occur	→ phenomenon

Sometimes, adjectives (such as *different* or *available*) are also turned into nouns (*difference, availability*), which can then be qualified (this *difference* in wind directions and speed; the *availability* of antibiotics in many countries). This process of turning verbs or adjectives into nouns is referred to by linguists as "nominalization."[8]

Nominalization turns actions (typically realized in verbs) or attributes (typically realized in adjectives) into "things" (typically realized in nouns). In so doing, it enables scientists to create theoretical or virtual entities that can then be observed, experimented with, and modified. For example, by turning the verb "survive" into the noun "survival," scientists are then able to expand it into *the survival of plants* by adding an article (*the*) before it and a prepositional phrase (*of plants*) after it. This allows scientists to establish a relationship between the two entities, light and plants, as *important* through the use of a linking verb (*is*). Similarly, the "de-verbal" nouns, *growth* and *development,* act as abstract entities in the scientific process of being regulated by hormones.

From a text organization perspective, nominalization enables scientists to synthesize what has been said in the prior discourse into a "thing" so that it becomes the subject of ensuing discussion. For example, *this phenomenon* in the last sentence of the excerpt recapitulates what was stated in the previous sentences (that is, interaction between light and plant) and becomes the starting point for the definition of phototropism. This way of using language helps create information flow in the text.

"De-verbal" and "de-adjectival" nouns, or nominalizations, embody abstractions from concrete actions or attributes. They facilitate the presentation of information and development of arguments. Heavy uses of this type of noun can be a source of reading difficulty for students. See, for example, the following excerpt from a seventh-grade science textbook, where the use of nominalizations (in bold) makes this short passage appear abstract and potentially taxing to process.

Plate tectonics is one process that causes changing environments on Earth. As plates on Earth's surface moved over time, continents collided with and separated from each other many times. **Continental collisions** caused **mountain building** and **the draining of seas**. **Continental separations** caused deeper seas to develop between continents. **This rearranging of land and sea** still causes changes in climates today.[9]

In this excerpt, *continental collisions* and *continental separations* are rewordings of the phrase *continents collided and separated*, which appeared in the previous sentence. The rewordings enable the author to continue the discussion of the same idea (that continents collided and continents separated) by making it the subjects of subsequent sentences. Similarly, *mountain building* and *the draining of seas* derive from the actions of "building mountains" and "draining seas." The nominalizations construct two abstract entities that are then put into a causal relation with another abstract entity (*continental collision*). Finally, the nominalization *this rearranging of land and sea* summarizes what has been discussed in the previous three sentences and serves as the subject of the last sentence. Understanding how nominalization works in scientific meaning making and discourse construction is an important reading skill students need to develop to effectively comprehend science texts.

Density

Another feature of the plant text is that it is packed with dense information. One way to gauge the informational density of a text is to calculate its lexical density, that is, the average number of content-carrying words per non-embedded clause. The higher the number, the denser the text. In order to compute the lexical density index, several linguistics terms need to be explained. First, content-carrying words (called lexical items) generally include nouns (*Arthur, plants*), verbs (*say, know*), adjectives (*slow, shady*), and some adverbs (*faster, suddenly*). Other words—such as articles (*the, a*), prepositions (*in, of*), pronouns (*they, it*), demonstratives (*that, these*), auxiliary verbs (*would* love, *is* playing), conjunctions (*and, when*), and some adverbs (*more, very*)—are called grammatical items. Second, a clause is, simply put, a grammatical unit that includes a verb and a subject (explicit or implied) and expresses a message; it is the central processing unit in the grammar and an information unit in a text.[10] Some sentences contain multiple verbs and thus have more than one clause. Table 2.2 identifies four major clause types in the English language. Main clause, coordinate clause, and subordinate clause are considered non-embedded clauses. Table 2.3 breaks down the Arthur and plant texts into non-embedded clauses.

Table 2.2   Major Clause Types in English[11]

Clause Types	Definition	Examples (underlined)
Main Clause	It is the only clause in a simple sentence, the initiating clause in a complex sentence with coordinate clauses, or the dominant clause in a complex sentence with subordinate clauses.	• Ads for the Treat Timer <u>were</u> everywhere. • "Gee, I'd love to help," <u>said Dad</u>, . . . • <u>Light is so important to the survival of plants</u> that they seem to reach toward it.
Coordinate Clause	It is linked to the main clause with a coordinating conjunction (like *and*) or merely juxtaposed (as in a direct quotation).	• Blake went to the beach <u>and</u> collected some shells. • "<u>Gee, I'd love to help</u>," said Dad.
Subordinate Clause	It is dependent on but not part of another clause. This category includes adverbial clauses (those introduced by *if, when, where, because, but*), nonrestrictive relative clause (typically introduced by *which* or *where* and preceded by a comma), and clauses projected through verbs of saying (*state, say, tell*) and thinking (*know, believe*).	• "I know <u>what you're thinking</u>," said D.W. • A plant may not have eyes to tell it <u>where the light is, but a plant does have hormones</u>. • Measuring longitude, <u>which relied on precise time-keeping</u>, was finally made possible in the 1760s with the development of accurate clocks called chronometers.
Embedded Clause	It is both dependent on and a part of another clause. It is typically introduced by a relative pronoun (*that, which, who, whose*) without a comma preceding it. The relative pronoun is sometimes left out.	• Auxins are hormones <u>that affect the growth of plant cells</u>. • The conclusions [that] <u>Mendel drew about how traits are inherited</u> still hold up today.

Table 2.3	Clauses in Arthur and Plant Texts

Arthur Text	Plant Text
1. **Ads** for the **Treat Timer** were **everywhere**.	1. **Light** is so **important** to the **survival** of **plants**
2. Now **Arthur** really **wanted** one.	2. that they seem to **reach** toward it.
3. **Arthur counted** his **money**.	3. But how does a **plant 'know'** which **way** to **grow**?
4. **D.W. helped**.	4. A **plant** may not **have eyes** to **tell** it
5. "Even with all of my **birthday money**," << . . . >> "I only **have ten dollars** and **three cents**."	5. where the **light** is,
6. << . . . , he **said**. . . . >>	6. but a **plant** does have **hormones**.
7. "I **know**	7. **Hormones** are **substances produced** by **plants** (and **animals**) that **regulate growth** and **development**.
8. what you're **thinking**,"	
9. **said D.W.**	8. **Auxins** are **hormones** that **affect** the **growth** of **plant cells**.
10. She **ran** to **protect** her **cash register**.	9. **Auxins cause cells** on the **shady side** of a **plant** to **grow faster** than **cells** on the **sunny side**.
11. **Arthur decided** to **ask Dad** for an **advance** on his **allowance**.	
12. "Gee, I'd **love** to **help**,"	10. As a **result**, a **plant's stem** may **bend** toward the **light**
13. **said Dad**,	
14. "but my **catering business is** a little **slow** right now."	11. to **allow** as much **light** as **possible** to **reach** the **maximum number** of **food-making cells**.
15. **Arthur knew**	
16. **Mom** would **understand**.	12. This **phenomenon** is **known** as **phototropism**.
17. "**Money** doesn't **grow** on **trees**,"	
18. **said Mother**,	
19. "and I **think**	
20. **Pal likes treats** from you, not a **machine**."	

Content-carrying words are bold faced.

As Table 2.3 shows, the Arthur text has a total of 54 content-carrying words in 20 non-embedded clauses, yielding a lexical density score of 2.7. The plant text, on the other hand, has 59 content-carrying words in 12 non-embedded clauses, yielding a lexical density score of 4.9. These numbers are consistent with what scholars have found regarding the informational density of everyday text versus the more specialized text of science. For example, according to applied linguist Michael Halliday,[12] in everyday spoken language there are two to three content-carrying words per clause, but in written language there are four to six content-carrying words per clause. In science, the number can go up much higher, often exceeding 10. The plant text here is almost two times as dense as the Arthur text. Some clauses in the plant text, such as *Hormones are substances produced by plants (and animals) that regulate growth and development* and *Auxins cause cells on the shady side of a plant to grow faster than cells on the sunny side,* contain as many as 8 and 11 content-carrying words (bold faced), respectively. Such a high density of information can create cognitive overload for students and slow down their processing of the text. To put these numbers in perspective, it must be noted that the lexical density of children's own writing is about three in primary grades (Grades 1–2), four to five in upper elementary grades (Grades 3–6), and six to seven in middle and high schools.[13] This shows that the texts school children are expected to read can be at a higher degree of informational density than the texts they are typically able to produce on their own.

The informational density of the plant text is achieved primarily through the use of long nouns. A comparison of the nouns in the two sample texts brings this to light (see Table 2.4). The nouns in the Arthur text, for example, are generally short and simple, consisting primarily of proper nouns (*Arthur, the Treat Timer, D.W.*) and pronouns (*I, he*). On the contrary, the plant text contains both short nouns (*light, they*) and long nouns (*the growth of plant cells; substances produced by plants and animals that regulate growth and development; the maximum number of food-making cells*). A long noun consists of a head with modifiers. Some modifiers come before the head and are called premodifiers; others are placed after the head and are called postmodifiers. For example, in *the maximum number of food-making cells,* the head *number* has two premodifiers—*the* (article) and *maximum* (adjective)—and a postmodifier *of food-making cells* (prepositional phrase). In *substances produced by plants and animals that regulate growth and development,* there is no premodifier; the head (*substances*) is postmodified by two embedded clauses, *[that are] produced by plants and animals [and] that regulate growth and development.*

Long nouns with embedded clauses are particularly useful in constructing scientific definitions, as they enable scientists to provide complete and accurate information about the concept being defined in terse, compact ways. This point can be illustrated with the following example from a seventh-grade science textbook, where two long

Table 2.4	Comparison of Nouns in Arthur and Plant Texts
Arthur Text	**Plant Text**
ads, the Treat Timer, Arthur, one, Arthur, his money, D.W., all of my birthday money, he, I, ten dollars, three cents, I, what, you, D.W., she, her cash register, Arthur, Dad, an advance on his allowance, I, Dad, my catering business, Arthur, Mom, money, trees, Mother, I, Pal, treats, you, a machine	light, the survival of plants, they, it, a plant, which way to grow, a plant, eyes, it, the light, a plant, hormones, hormones, substances produced by plants (and animals) that regulate growth and development, auxins, hormones that affect the growth of plant cells, auxins, cells on the shady side of a plant, cells on the sunny side, a result, a plant's stem, the light, as much light as possible, the maximum number of food-making cells, this phenomenon, phototropism

nouns (italicized) with embedded clauses (bold faced) are used to define the technical concept of plankton.

> Plankton are *tiny marine algae and animals* **that drift with currents**. Most algae plankton are *one-celled organisms* **that float in the upper layers of the ocean where light needed for photosynthesis is found**.[14]

Note that in the italicized portion of the second sentence, the head *organisms* is premodified with an adjectival phrase (*one-celled*) and postmodified with an embedded clause, *that float in the upper layers of the ocean*, which is itself further modified with another embedded clause, *where light needed for photosynthesis is found*. Such multilayered modification results in a long, complex noun that presents a significant obstacle to comprehension.

We can also compare the average length of nouns in the Arthur and plant texts. In the Arthur text, each noun averages 1.5 words. The plant text averages about 3.0 words per noun, which is two times as high as the Arthur text. Recall that the plant text is also about two times as dense as the Arthur text. This suggests that nouns are probably the most powerful grammatical resource that contributes to a text's informational density.[15] One reason for this is that English nouns can be expanded almost indefinitely, allowing the text writer to add information when needed. Because more data are being packed into nouns in the science text than in the

> *Because more data are being packed into nouns in the science text than in the storybook text, when children read science texts they have to process more information at the clause level.*

storybook text, when children read science texts they have to process more information at the clause level. For this reason, scholars have suggested that the ability to handle long nouns is an important reading skill students need to develop in order to successfully interact with science texts.[16]

Metaphorical Realizations of Logical Reasoning

An additional feature of the plant text is that logical reasoning is sometimes construed metaphorically. In storybook language and everyday spoken language, logical connections among ideas are typically realized explicitly between clauses through a few common conjunctions, such as *and, and then, if, but, when, because,* and *so.* This is the case with the following excerpt from Linda Urban's *A Crooked Kind of Perfect,* a popular novel for Grades 3 through 5.

> People have shifted all the chairs around in Meeting Room G and there's not much of an aisle left, so I have to weave around people to get to the front of the room where the judges are. And when I get there I hand them my music, but I still have my competition packet in my hands.[17]

The same can be said about the Arthur text, where the conjunctions *but* and *and* are used to explicitly connect the ideas in the dialogues.

In science texts, however, logical reasoning is not always conveyed through conjunctions. It can also be realized through nouns, verbs, and prepositional phrases. This makes logical connections among ideas implicit and more difficult for students to discern. For example, instead of using conjunctions such as *because* and *so,* the plant text uses two verbs (*affect, cause*) and a noun (*a result*) to signal causal relations between auxins and the growth of plant cells. This reasoning within, rather than between, clauses facilitates the construction of logical relations between technical concepts. Examples of such within-clause reasoning (italicized) abound in both science textbooks[18] and trade books[19]:

- For many people, the amazing beauty of animals in the wild is *the reason* to protect them. (the reason = because)
- *With* the emergence of new diseases, however, antiquated ways of thinking sometimes take hold. (with = despite)

- The changes occurring today, however, are primarily *the result* of human activity. (the result = because)
- The presence of mountain ranges also has *an effect* on rainfall patterns. (the effect = because . . . so)
- In temperate zones, weather generally changes *with* the season. (with = because of)
- As Earth moves around the sun, different areas of Earth tilt toward the sun, *bringing* different seasons. (bringing = so this brings)

Clearly, understanding how logical reasoning is construed in science is another reading skill that is key to the successful comprehension of science texts.

Impersonal Authoritativeness

Finally, unlike the Arthur text, which sounds interpersonal and involving in part because of its use of everyday vocabulary and inclusion of human dialogues, the plant text sounds much more distanced, impersonal, and authoritative. These features are realized through the use of a number of grammatical devices, including the following:

- Technical vocabulary (*auxins, phototropism*), which conveys specialized knowledge of science.
- Declarative sentences (*Light is so important to the survival of plants that they seem to reach toward it.*), which present information in an assertive manner. Note that interrogative sentences—such as *But how does a plant 'know' which way to grow?*—are occasionally used in school and popular sciences to stimulate the reader's interest in the topic. They are, however, rarely used in professional science. Imperative sentences, such as *Place the tube on the table,* are common in texts that give directions or instructions but rare in other types of science texts.
- Passive voice (*is known*), which enables a focus on "things" and gives the text a flavor of objectivity by enabling the suppression of human actors and other agents behind the scientific processes.
- Theoretical or virtual entities made of abstract and lengthy nouns (*this phenomenon, substances produced by plants and animals that regulate growth and development*), which make the text appear detached from the lived experiences of children's everyday world.

These linguistic devices enable scientists to present information accurately, objectively, and assertively. Because of its impersonal authoritativeness, the plant text appears both less involving and more alienating. This is contrary to the Arthur text, where the reader tends to feel more comfortable with the familiar and interactive language through which the story is constructed.

The following example on measurement from a sixth-grade science textbook presents another instance of impersonal authoritativeness in school science. This short excerpt contains technical vocabulary (*latitude, longitude, elevation, velocity*), passive voice (*is used, can be determined, are used*), abstract nouns (*this measurement, accuracy, corrections*), and long nouns (*the time it takes for the receiver to communicate with each satellite; receivers at ground-based stations with fixed positions*). These grammatical patterns differ significantly from those typically used in storybook texts and render the excerpt more difficult to comprehend.

> The GPS (global positioning system) measures the time it takes for the receiver to communicate with each satellite. This measurement is used to calculate latitude, longitude, and elevation. If the receiver is moving, its velocity also can be determined. Receivers at ground-based stations with fixed positions are used to check accuracy and to make corrections for errors.[20]

CONCLUSION

Scientific texts use a range of grammatical features—technical, abstract, dense, impersonal, authoritative, and metaphorical—that present unique comprehension challenges for students. Teachers who understand how scientific meanings are constructed through language are in a better position to anticipate and diagnose students' reading/writing difficulties and to more effectively help them handle these difficulties.

> *Teachers who understand how scientific meanings are constructed through language are in a better position to anticipate and diagnose students' reading/writing difficulties.*

There has been much speculation as to what causes children's reading achievement to drop in the intermediate grades, especially when compared with the robust reading growth that occurs in the primary grades. Some have suggested that this notorious "fourth-grade slump" phenomenon can be explained in part by the shift from the story-heavy curriculum in the primary grades to a more expository-oriented curriculum in later years of schooling.[21] Our comparative analysis of the Arthur and plant texts in this chapter helps explain why students in the intermediate grades may find the expository texts in content areas like science challenging. To help students become proficient readers of science, teachers must (a) provide opportunities for them to read lots of science texts, (b) equip them with tools for coping with the new demands of scientific language, and (c) scaffold their interaction with texts through strategy instruction. These three components are taken up in Chapters 3, 4, and 5, respectively.

We recognize that today's science texts are often multimodal and multisemiotic, containing not just verbal language but also mathematics and visual representations. However, it is primarily through written language that scientific knowledge has historically been constructed, stored, and transmitted.[22] It is also primarily through written texts (like textbooks, trade books, and magazines) that students are apprenticed into school science. For these reasons, a major focus on the written language of science (that is, science texts) is warranted. As Australian literacy educator Robert Veel has argued,

> Although spoken language, images and physical activity all play an important part in producing meaning in school science, historically it has been written language which has played a central role in the construction, production, reproduction and dissemination of scientific meaning . . . This continues to be the case today, even though the physical appearance of written texts has altered radically in recent years and the teaching of science exclusively through written textbooks has become unfashionable classroom practice.[23]

Readers who are interested in learning about how to read multimodal and multisemiotic texts in science are encouraged to consult the work of, for example, Jay Lemke, Gunther Kress, Len Unsworth, Kay O'Halloran, and Vaughan Prain.[24]

3

Using Trade Books to Support Science Inquiry

As noted in Chapter 2, one of the pillars of reading comprehension is background knowledge. Extensive research suggests that background knowledge, which includes both mundane and specialized knowledge, provides much of the basis for text comprehension and recall.[1] Lacking background knowledge about the topic of a text can hinder the reader's effort to construct a coherent mental representation of the text,[2] which is essential to text comprehension, learning, and engagement.

Given the role of background knowledge in reading comprehension and in learning in general, it is clear that science teachers need to have a content-rich curriculum through which students can build up their store of knowledge about science. One way to help students expand their content knowledge in science and to support inquiry-based science is to have them engage in wide reading of science-related reading materials. In this chapter, we focus on one important kind of science reading materials—science trade books—that have recently become a popular resource in the science classroom. We explain the rationale for infusing trade books into the science curriculum, describe key resources for finding quality science trade books, identify some of the additional skills needed for reading science trade books (beyond those discussed in Chapter 2), and describe the many ways that trade books can be used to support the teaching of science as inquiry.

WHY READ TRADE BOOKS IN SCIENCE?

There are many advantages for infusing trade books into the science curriculum. Trade books usually provide more depth than textbooks in their treatment of science topics. A topic that is typically covered in a few textbook paragraphs or pages, such as limestone or waves, becomes the subject of an entire trade book. Trade books can afford to go beyond "declarations of 'fact'"[3] and include a lot more background information, illustrations, quantitative and qualitative data, explanations, and concrete examples. They also provide information (such as an exploration of faraway rainforests) that cannot be obtained through the firsthand classroom experience of experiments and observations. In so doing, trade books enable students to build up rich content knowledge about science and develop interpretive skills that support scientific inquiries.

In addition, trade books portray science as it is practiced in the real world, showing how scientists formulate questions and seek answers to these questions through both hands-on (firsthand) and minds-on (secondhand) explorations. As such, trade books provide good models of inquiry science and can stimulate students' interest in conducting scientific inquiries of their own. They also help students recognize that science is a very human activity, full of accidents and biases and not always "clean, exact, certain, definitive, unequivocal, and uncontested."[4]

> Trade books portray science as it is practiced in the real world, showing how scientists formulate questions and seek answers to these questions.

Because trade books can cover many different topics in greater depth, they are often more interesting to read. They are also more accessible than textbooks, especially outside of school. With the broad range of trade books available on science topics today, it is possible to find quality books that have special appeal to all students in a class. When students find books of interest, they are more likely to read—and learn from—them. And as students become experts in the subject they read about, they often like to share their knowledge with their peers. This can be motivating and empowering for students, leading them to develop healthy reading habits, which are essential to becoming lifelong learners of science.

Another advantage of trade books is that they are better able to accommodate the needs of students with varying reading abilities. Often, there are many different trade books on the same topic that are written at different reading levels. Students who are proficient readers can read science content in books that are complex and learn at their own rate. This kind of learning is satisfying and prevents students from feeling bored in school. At the other end of the spectrum, students who are reading below grade level can also use appropriate books with substantive science content.

In short, trade books are an important resource in science learning. They provide up-to-date, in-depth information on a wide variety of science topics and are ideal for building students' content knowledge about science. They are more likely than textbooks to engage students, promote inquiry learning, and foster critical thinking. A science curriculum that infuses trade books is "richer, more coherent, and more authentic" than one without trade books.[5]

AWARD-WINNING SCIENCE TRADE BOOKS

Each year, many trade books on science topics are published, but not all of them are well written or contain accurate information. Because what students read has a significant impact on what they learn, their attitudes toward learning, and how they write and think,[6] teachers need to make sure that the books they select for inclusion in the science curriculum are of high quality in both content and writing.

But where can teachers find quality science trade books? The best way to find excellent books on science topics is by seeking out books that win awards. Several professional organizations give annual awards and honors that recognize outstanding science trade books. Books that win these awards are usually chosen by committees made up of scientists, educators, and librarians.

For example, the National Science Teachers Association (NSTA), in cooperation with the Children's Book Council, creates an annual list of about 40 quality science books for children and young adults called the NSTA Outstanding Science Trade Books for Students K–12. The list is published in the March issue of *Science and Children* (for teachers of Grades K–6) and *Science Scope* (for teachers of Grades 6–9) and is placed on the NSTA website (www.nsta.org). The books are sorted into topical areas, such as archaeology, anthropology, and paleontology; biography; earth and space science; environment and ecology; fiction; life science; physical science; science-related careers; and technology and engineering. They are also identified according to the National Science

Content Standards, which are unifying concepts and processes, science as inquiry, physical science perspectives, life science, earth and space science, science and technology, science in personal and social perspectives, and the history and nature of science. In addition, the reading level for each book is provided: P = Primary (Grades K–2); E = Elementary (Grades 3–5); I = Intermediate (Grades 6–8); A = Advanced (Grades 9–12). These levels are intended only as guidelines and not meant to limit the potential uses of the books.

Besides NSTA, other organizations also create their own lists of quality science trade books. For example, the American Association for the Advancement of Science (AAAS), with support from Subaru America Inc., created the AAAS/Subaru SB & F Prize for Excellence in Science Books in 2005 to celebrate outstanding science writing and illustration for children and young adults. The prize is awarded to books in four categories—children's science picture books, middle grades nonfiction science books, popular science for high school readers, and hands-on science/activity books. The award winners can be found at the AAAS website (www.aaas.org).

The National Council of Teachers of English (NCTE) established the Orbis Pictus Award for Outstanding Nonfiction for Children in 1990 to recognize books that demonstrate excellence in the writing of nonfiction for children. The award is given annually to one informational book published in America during the previous year. Many science books win this award. Although only one title is singled out for the award, up to five titles are also recognized as Honor Books each year. It is thus important to examine not just the award winners but the total list, which is available from the NCTE website (www.ncte.org).

The Association for Library Service to Children (ALSC), with support from Bound to Stay Bound Books, Inc., created the Robert F. Sibert Informational Book Award in 2001 to honor authors whose nonfiction work has made a significant contribution to the field of children's literature. The award is presented annually to the most distinguished informational book published in English during the previous year. The award winners can be found on the website of the American Library Association (www.ala.org).

BECOMING FAMILIAR WITH THE FORMAT OF SCIENCE TRADE BOOKS

Science trade books, particularly the nonfiction ones, are usually presented in a format different from storybooks. They include features such as illustrations or pictures, table of contents, glossaries, thesaurus, index, charts, graphs, and maps. This new format requires that students develop additional reading skills (beyond those discussed in Chapter 2) for handling science trade books. These skills include

- finding information about authors and illustrators;
- examining a table of contents, index, and glossary;
- interpreting illustrations, captions, charts, graphs, and maps; and
- using a bibliography or source notes to verify information.

Each of these skills is elaborated below.

Finding Information About Authors and Illustrators

Students need to be aware that science trade books are written by real people and these people often have a purpose for writing their books. An author's background, experience, purpose, and perspective all influence what he chooses to write about, the information he selects to include, and the way he presents that information in the book. A good book will provide the author's credentials and writing processes, either on the back flap of the book or on a page before or after the main part of the book. If it does not, an Internet search should yield information about the author, as book publishers often include a website for their authors and many authors also have their own websites. Information about authors can also be found in a library reference book series called "Something About the Author" (over 200 volumes to date) published by Gale, which is a division of Cengage Learning. Each volume in the series provides illustrated biographical profiles of roughly 75 children's authors and artists, with each profile containing information about the individual's personal life, contact details, career highlights, complete bibliography, and works in progress.

Illustrations in science trade books often provide information that is just as important as the information conveyed through words. Thus, it is important to find out the qualifications of illustrators. Many illustrators are artists beyond just illustrating books and maintain their own websites. These illustrators create artistically beautiful illustrations, but they are not always accurate. Book publishers sometimes include illustrator information on their websites, where the reader can view other examples by the illustrator and learn about how the artist creates scientifically accurate illustrations.

Examining a Table of Contents, Index, and Glossary

A science trade book typically has a table of contents that provides an overview of the topics covered in the book. Teachers can make reference to the table of contents every time they share a book until students know automatically to consult this page to determine what they will be reading. Consulting the table of contents lets students know immediately if there is anything in the book that is related to the information they are seeking. Alternatively, students can create a table of contents for a group project where each student has created one section of the work. For example, for a group or class book about birds, each student or group can find information and write about a different bird. This type of book is a collection and would need a table of contents that lists the title and the author of each piece.

Another useful feature of nonfiction informational books is the index. Once students have searched the table of contents for general topics in the book, they can then use the index as a directory to help them find specific topics. The skills needed to capitalize on what an index has to offer are alphabetizing and using a thesaurus. Most computers have a thesaurus in their tool bar. Once students discover the use of synonyms, they will know how to make the most of an index.

A glossary, an alphabetical list of technical terms and their meanings, can be an important aide to understanding text information. Referring to a glossary while reading informational science books is a useful skill to acquire. Students can learn to create glossaries in their own writing of, for example, informational reports.

Referring to a glossary while reading informational science books is a useful skill to acquire.

Interpreting Illustrations, Captions, Charts, Graphs, and Maps

Illustrations in science trade books serve two functions—to provide information and to attract readers. Science trade books are illustrated in many different media, including photography, paint, mixed media, and sketches. Here, two considerations are paramount: size and accuracy. Many science trade books, especially those that cram a lot of information into one book (such as encyclopedic books), provide up-close illustrations, which can distort students' perception of the size of the organism or object depicted. Even photography sometimes isolates features. Illustrators like Dennis Kunkel use microphotography, or illustrations of microscopic organisms. Those need to be identified with the degree of magnification.

Science illustrations need to incorporate authentic colors. It is easy to alter photographs to make them interesting and creative, but that can affect the quality of the science information provided. Some illustrators create fanciful pictures that add creativity to science writing but compromise the accuracy of the information presented. For example, animals can appear larger, more colorful, or in more exotic environments than where they actually live. Teaching students to recognize style issues such as proportional size and authentic color can make them better readers of illustrated science books.

Most readers become enthralled by the illustrations in a science trade book and neglect to examine the captions, which often contain vital information for interpreting the illustrations. Simply alerting students to the captions should do the trick. Asking students to caption their own artwork or science displays will also help them recognize the value of captions when reading the work of others.

A considerable amount of information in science trade books is synthesized in charts, graphs, or maps. Thus, it is important for students to develop skills in interpreting these visual elements. Teachers can chart data from student reports so that the whole class can see how to create a chart (or graph). Students can graph the data they have gathered from any scientific activity. By charting or graphing their own data, students quickly learn to interpret the charts and graphs in books.

Maps can be more difficult to read without instruction, and there are many different kinds of maps. Starting with the more familiar state road maps, which can be obtained at a minimal cost, students can graduate to other kinds of maps congruent with the science curriculum. Learning about directions, symbols, and scale on maps is a skill students will be able to use not just in science but also throughout their lifetime.

Using a Bibliography or Source Notes to Verify Information

A bibliography or source note tells readers where the author found the information presented in a book. Sources are especially important if the author is not a scientist. Identifying the source of information is also important because organizations and groups have special values and interests. For example, the National Wildlife

Federation, whose mission is to inspire Americans to protect wildlife for our children's future, publishes the popular science magazine, *Ranger Rick*. However, the organization is also a major gun lobby in Washington and supports hunting. Students can verify whether the information included in a book is accurate and unbiased by cross-checking with other sources.

USING TRADE BOOKS
TO EMPOWER SCIENCE LEARNING

There are many ways that trade books can be used to enhance students' learning experience in science. These include

- unit study using informational books,
- studying science and scientists through biographical literature,
- poetry studies,
- reading aloud,
- book study groups, and
- science author studies.

Unit Study Using Informational Books

One way to share trade books in the science class is to conduct units of study around important science topics. Having students read and discuss related science trade books in addition to firsthand explorations and field trips can enrich students' experiences and increase their learning and engagement in a unit, as trade books are a valuable resource for generating inquiry questions about a topic, seeking answers to these questions, gathering and verifying information, and stimulating enthusiasm about the topic.

To broaden the study of trade books on science topics, teachers can divide the class into groups and provide each group with several books on their topic of study. The students within each group can share their books and talk about what they are learning and wondering. Each group can also make a poster or present a PowerPoint to the class about what they have learned from their books and what questions they would like to further explore.

More creative ways of book sharing can be used as well. For example, William Straits and Sherry Nichols suggest that students can role play a trial after reading and discussing trade books about sharks.[7] For the role play, students are divided into several groups

(A, B, C, D). Group A acts as prosecuting attorneys depicting sharks as ferocious, cold-blooded killers with hundreds of razor-sharp teeth; Group B acts as defense attorneys suggesting that less than 10% of all shark species are known to attack humans; Group C acts as the jury who will weigh evidence from both sides and render a verdict on whether sharks should be condemned to the penitentiary; and Group D acts as witnesses in their roles as a seal, a whale, and a marine biologist. Through reading, discussing, dramatizing, and sharing their books, students gain deeper understanding of scientific concepts and develop greater enthusiasm for inquiry and learning.

Studying Science and Scientists Through Biographical Literature

Science teachers often include the study of scientists in their curriculum to help students understand that science is a human endeavor and that science is an exciting career. Many students often think of a scientist as a man with glasses in a white lab coat working in a lab. Reading science biographies enables students to deepen their understanding of the nature of science and to broaden their perceptions of scientists as they learn about real scientists' life stories, their involvement with science, and what personal and professional attributes contribute to their success.

Each year, many biographies of scientists are published, and some feature minority and women scientists. Biographies come in different forms. Some biographies cover the entire life span of a scientist and others only an important part of a scientist's life. There are nonfiction biographies (where everything is true) and fictionalized biographies (based on a real person but told as an entertaining story). Sometimes, a biography is embedded in an historical account of an important scientific invention or breakthrough. A good biography is well researched and engagingly written.

When reading a biography, it is important to keep in mind that the author of the book has a distinctive perspective on the scientist's life. Students need to critically read the literature by exploring the author's relationship to the scientist in the biography and how the author has gathered information for the book (such as interviews, document research, and/or personal knowledge). Validating any content through Internet sources is advised. Reading a good biography is a great precursor to having each student in a class select a different scientist, conduct research to write about the scientist's life, and share the information with classmates.

One creative way to use biographies in the science classroom is to have students read biographies and then present an interactive historical vignette about the scientist of their choice.[8] Each student writes a short vignette about a major event in a scientist's life, dresses like the scientist, bring props representing the scientist's work, and reads the vignette in small groups. The "scientist" then asks her peer "scientists" for opinions about her invention(s).

Another way of using biographies is to have students select a quote from one of their favorite scientists (see, for example, www.quotationspage.com) and then write either an explanation of what it means or a personal response to it. This activity can enhance students' understanding of a particular science concept, science process, scientific habit of mind, or science career. In short, reading, discussing, and writing about scientists of personal interest can help students develop an appreciation for the nature of science, demystify science as something only for the genius, and attract them to consider a career in science.

Poetry Studies

Another way of infusing trade books in the science classroom is to share poetry books that contain accurate science content. Like science, poetry is a way of knowing about the world that involves making careful observations, forming connections, and evoking an empathic response.[9] One way to combine science and poetry is to have students determine the scientific accuracy of a poem. Teachers can also have students read, discuss, and develop poems on a science topic (like insects) as a way of introducing them to a research project involving the topic.[10]

In addition, teachers can zero in on the creative voice of poetry to enhance the study of science. For example, Robert King described how poetry can be integrated into the study of environmental science.[11] Students read and respond to William Stafford's poems, create a Google Earth literature trip (http://www.google littrips.org), write their own environmental poems, discuss the role of a poet in caring for the earth, and compose photo essays about the planet.

Finally, when students have read and enjoyed poems, they can hold a poetry jam in their class by reading and performing poems (or parts of poems) for the class. Some of the poems are written in two voices and can be performed by two people. Students might also be inspired to write their own science poems.

Reading Aloud

Reading aloud provides teachers with an opportunity to model how to read informational books and to demonstrate their enthusiasm about science and books. It also helps make science less intimidating, increases students' background knowledge and science vocabulary, keeps their natural curiosity about science alive, and motivates them to do extension activities such as reading additional books to learn more about the topic, conducting hands-on inquiries to test hypotheses or verify text information, and writing reports for sharing with the class.

When selecting books for read-alouds, it is important to make sure that the books are engagingly written and enjoyable to hear and that the topic is of interest to students. Books with large, colorful illustrations are also appropriate for reading to a class. Many of the award-winning books discussed earlier in this chapter are good candidates for read alouds in the classroom. Book Links, a web-based resource from the American Library Association (http://www.ala.org/ala/aboutala/offices/publishing/booklinks/index.cfm), provides an annotated list of books for science read-alouds. Some of these books (like picture books) can be read in just one sitting, while others (such as chapter books) might best be read on several different days. During read-alouds, the teacher keeps good eye contact with students; models expressive reading, scientific thinking, and problem solving; examines photographs and illustrations; clarifies and explains abstract concepts; encourages conversation and wondering; and generates questions for discussion and investigation.

A five-step model proposed by Charlotte Zales and Connie Unger helps teachers plan effective read-alouds to support science learning.[12] The first step is for the teacher to review the trade book selection through a science lens and determine whether the science content (subject matter, topic) of the book is relevant and appropriate to the curriculum. In Steps 2 and 3, the teacher identifies what literacy processes (reading skills readers use to construct meaning, such as predicting, inferring, questioning, and visualizing) and science processes (inquiry skills scientists use for investigation, such as predicting, observing, experimenting, inferring, classifying, modeling, and communicating) are demonstrated in the book. Next, the teacher decides what teaching strategies to use before, during, and after reading the trade book, keeping in mind the target content and process skills identified earlier. Finally, the teacher determines how the book can lead to further science inquiries such as conducting a demonstration, taking a field trip, reading additional books and materials, writing a personal response or a formal report, and designing an experiment.

Book Study Groups

Book study groups can broaden and deepen the study of science content in school; they also give students ownership of their learning. Once a week throughout the year, students check out a book from the classroom or school library to read in class or at home and then gather in small groups to share with their peers the information they have learned and the questions they have formulated from the books. Students can then exchange books so that good books travel around the classroom and into students' homes. Each group can also develop presentations about their books to share with the entire class. Sometimes, students in the same group can read a common book and share their responses to that book.

One way of organizing book study groups is to have students form "literature circles."[13] Members of each book study group assume a different role, such as those identified below by William Straits:

1. Everyday life connector—to identify objects, organisms, characters, events, ideas, or concepts that remind students of their everyday life;

2. Science skeptic—to critically analyze how science is done in the book;

3. Power investigator—to identify which character in the book has the political, social, economic, or intellectual power to influence science;

4. Science translator—to define technical science vocabulary and concepts in the book by using glossaries, dictionaries, textbooks, or Internet;

5. Historian—to search for other scientific breakthroughs that happen at the same time, if a scientific discovery of the past is mentioned in the book;

6. Science biographer—to use textbook or Internet to find biographical information about significant individuals (particularly scientists) mentioned in the book;

7. Nature of science investigator—to look in the book for examples that accurately describe science (e.g., science is not merely mechanistic, but a creative process; scientific knowledge is uncertain and can change over time; science cannot provide complete answers to all questions);

8. Science and culture connector—to consider how culture influences science development in the past and at present.[14]

When students read, they perform their assigned roles and take notes to support their participation in the group discussion.

To ensure the success of book study groups, teachers need to provide students with many quality science trade books on a wide range of science topics. They also need to provide time in class for students to read and share books. If class time is limited, students can do most of the reading at home, in which case it is important for the teacher to communicate regularly with parents to solicit their support. A home science reading program that encourages students to read and share books with family members and friends is described in an article by Zhihui Fang and his colleagues.[15]

Science Author Studies

There are many outstanding authors of science trade books. These include professional writers of books on science topics (James M. Deem, Kelly Milner Halls, Laurie Lindop, Debbie S. Miller, Sy Montgomery, Andrew K. Revkin, Seymour Simon, Darlene R. Stille), professional writers of biographies of scientists (Marfe Ferguson Delano, Lorraine Jean Hopping, Kathleen Krull, Phillip Steele, Catherine Thimmesh), authors who are scientists (David Burnie, Nicola Davies, Lesley Dendy, Jeanette Farrell, Phillip Hoose, Sandra Markle, Adrienne Mason, Dorothy Hinshaw Patent, Alvin and Virginia Silverstein), and artists who write about science (Jim Arnosky, Joan Harris, Ron Miller, Richard Platt, Christopher Sloan). Many of these individuals are recognized for their excellent work by relevant professional organizations. For example, Jim Arnosky, Patricia Lauber, Laurence Pringle, and Seymour Simon are four of the most prolific science trade book authors or author-illustrators who have been given the lifetime achievement award by the American Association for the Advancement of Science (AAAS). Table 3.1 lists some of the science trade book authors who have won the prestigious Washington Post/Children's Book Guild Nonfiction Award, which honors an author or author-illustrator whose total work has made significant contributions to informational books for children.

Table 3.1	Science Winners of the Washington Post/Children's Book Guild Nonfiction Award	

Date	Author	Book Topics
1977	David Macaulay	castle, cathedral (design and architecture)
1983	Patricia Lauber	over 100 books with many science topics
1985	Isaac Asimov	many science topics
1988	Jim Arnosky	nature, wildlife, environment, "Backyard Safari" TV Series
1993	Seymour Simon	over 200 books with many topics, photo illustrations
1998	Jean C. George	nature, animals, environment
1999	Laurence Pringle	over 100 books with many topics (including natural history and science)
2001	Jim Murphy	science events in history
2004	Dorothy H. Patent	nature, animals
2005	Caroline Arnold	many areas of science
2006	Sneed B. Collard III	animals, nature
2010	Sy Montgomery	nature, animals

In science author study, students read multiple books by one author and discuss the author's writing style and book creation process. Each author has individual strategies for sharing information with young people. Through author study, students gain insights into how an author's background and life experience shape his writing style and creative process.

> *In science author study, students read multiple books by one author and discuss the author's writing style and book creation process.*

Authors who write more than one book on a science topic are especially suitable for author studies. The author study could come after students have had the opportunity to read quite a few books and have become acquainted with quite a few authors. Students can look up an author they enjoy on the Internet. If they can find information about the author, they should read at least one other book by the same individual and prepare a report for the class so that many authors are highlighted during the unit.

CONCLUSION

Science trade books play an important role in science teaching and learning. They present information about a variety of science topics in greater depth and more appealing ways than textbooks. They can take students on vicarious journeys (to outer space, faraway jungles, or ocean floors) that cannot otherwise be provided in firsthand classroom investigations. They also give students exposure to the language of science. As such, science trade books are a major resource for engaging students in the learning process, for broadening and deepening the curricular content, and for providing good models of science writing. Through reading and discussing trade books, students are able to ask questions; generate, clarify, and share ideas; make hypotheses; propose explanations; examine alternative explanations; draw conclusions; and conduct further inquiries. Teachers who find ways to infuse trade books into their curriculum are in a better position to develop students' science literacy in both the fundamental and the derived senses.

4

Learning Language, Learning Science

As we demonstrated in Chapter 2, scientific knowledge and understanding is constructed with a special kind of language that differs from the storybook language of the primary grades and the language children use to socialize in their everyday life. Scientific language evolved from everyday spoken language to meet the needs of modern Western science;[1] it enables scientists to think and reason in ways that facilitate the development of new theories and dissemination of new knowledge. Learning to read and write science thus requires students to learn the "peculiar" grammar that scientists use to construct and communicate knowledge. It is for this reason that learning science is often equated with learning the language of science.[2] As Wellington and Osborne affirmed, " . . . teaching about the use of language of science is not an optional extra but central to the process of learning science."[3]

One of the reasons why many students feel uncomfortable with the expository language of science is that they are rarely exposed to it. Studies of the literacy practices in primary-grade classrooms have reported that students in the early years of schooling engaged in very little expository reading and writing (that is, reading and writing texts in the nonfiction genres of procedure, description, report, explanation, and argumentation). For example, American literacy researcher Nell Duke studied 20 first-grade classrooms selected from very low- and very high-socioeconomic school districts in the Boston,

Massachusetts, area.[4] She found that there were few informational texts included in classroom libraries, little informational text on classroom walls and other surfaces, and a mean of only 3.6 minutes per day spent with informational texts during classroom activities involving written language. Findings from other studies have also confirmed the underuse of informational texts in the elementary school,[5] despite the recent push for teachers to include more expository texts in the classroom.[6] This lack of experience with expository texts can jeopardize children's literacy development. As Australian literacy educator Beverly Derewianka pointed out,

> *Lack of experience with expository texts can jeopardize children's literacy development.*

> When children are immersed in spoken language and written texts which are relatively close to spoken language, the transition to the sort of adult written texts marked by density, nominalisation and lengthy nominal groups may not always be as straightforward as we sometimes assume. This might help explain why older children often appear to have difficulties understanding their secondary textbooks. While all children need exposure to a wide range of genres, older children in particular need to engage with well-written texts which provide demonstrations of features of compactly structured writing.[7]

Another reason for students' struggle with science texts may be a lack of explicit instruction in the art of expository reading.[8] Reading instruction in content areas such as science has traditionally focused on basic skills (like decoding, fluency, predicting, summarizing, inferencing, visualizing) and generalizable strategies (such as note taking, thinking aloud), with little or no attention to the specific language demands (other than vocabulary) presented in these texts. As a result, many preadolescent and adolescent students often do not differentiate between reading narrative and expository texts.[9] While most students in the intermediate grades have few problems with basic skills such as decoding, fluency, predicting, and inferencing, many of them show a limited repertoire of coping strategies when reading the more demanding texts in content areas like science. It is thus imperative that teachers incorporate language-based tasks in their science lessons. As Yore and Treagust have suggested, "Learning how to talk, write, and read science frequently requires the embedding of explicit language tasks and instruction into science inquiry."[10]

BUILDING A LANGUAGE-RICH
SCIENCE CURRICULUM

One way to increase students' ability to handle science texts is to expose them to lots of these texts and invite them to read them. Studies have shown, however, that students are seldom given time to read independently in school[11] and that content teachers often require students to read very little text.[12] Instead, some science teachers focus on hands-on activities of observation and experiments and rarely use written texts in instruction. Others provide students with PowerPoint summaries of the information presented in the textbook instead of requiring students to read the material on their own.

Another common practice recommended for science teachers is to give students less challenging materials in the form of informational storybooks, which present science topics in a story format (with setting, problem, resolution). While these texts can help stimulate students' interest in science, they should not supplant the more prototypic expository texts. If students have little experience reading expository texts, they will not be prepared to handle the more demanding reading materials that are required of them in later years of schooling. Teachers need to provide systematic opportunities for students to read widely through, for example, a home science reading program that encourages students to check out books to read, respond to, discuss, and share on a regular basis.[13] It is important that students read not only textbooks but also other materials such as nonfiction trade books, popular science books, and science journals and magazines. These resources provide authentic expository language that prepares students to deal with the language demands of schooling.

Providing students access to quality reading materials with authentic expository language is a necessary, but often insufficient, condition for improving students' ability to handle the more demanding science texts beyond the primary grades. Many students do not get used to the specialized language of science through mere exposure. They also need to be able to understand, appreciate, and eventually appropriate the grammatical choices that scientists typically make in presenting information, constructing values and worldviews, and structuring discourse. In the rest of this chapter, we describe a number of language-based tasks for enabling the development of this ability. These tasks are grouped into three categories based on our discussion of the linguistic challenges of science texts in Chapter 2: those dealing with technical vocabulary, those dealing with abstract and dense nouns, and those dealing with discourse-level challenges.

DEVELOPING VOCABULARY KNOWLEDGE

One of the greatest challenges in learning science is learning its technical vocabulary. For this reason, we describe five tasks for building students' knowledge of science vocabulary. These are morphemic analysis, vocabulary think chart, concept definition word map, vocabulary self-collection, and word sort.

Morphemic Analysis

A morpheme is the smallest meaningful unit of a written language. In morphemic analysis, a word, such as *desalination,* is broken up into its smallest meaningful units: prefix (*de-*), root (or base) word (*saline*), and suffix (*-ate, -ion*). Once the meanings of these smallest parts become known, the meaning of the whole word can then be figured out.

The classification system used in modern Western science is based on the work of Greek scholar Aristotle and Swedish scientist Carolus Linnaeus, who used Latin words in his naming system. This means that technical terms in science often have Greek or Latin origins. As such, they are typically multimorphemic. Direct instruction of roots and affixes (prefix and suffix) can help students develop control over the technical vocabulary of science and promote a more precise understanding of science.

Despite their importance to learning the technical vocabulary of science, affixes and roots are rarely given sufficient attention in science lessons. For example, in a study of middle school teachers' practices in teaching key vocabulary in science and geography, British researcher Penelope Robinson found that "the teaching of vocabulary focused exclusively on meaning, rather than on the structure of the words, with the result that the pupils often developed some conceptual understanding of words which they were unable to express linguistically."[14] Robinson argued that it is important for students, especially English language learners, to develop not only semantic knowledge of the vocabulary but also the syntactic and morphological word knowledge. She recommended "additional, decontextualised, language-focused teaching of vocabulary" by directly drawing students' attention to the morphological and syntactic features of key words and introducing relevant affixes and roots (or base words).[15] She further suggested that subject-specific vocabulary teaching that integrates language study with subject knowledge ensures that students not only understand but are also able to use science vocabulary.

Some of the more common prefixes, suffixes, and roots for Grades 3 to 8 science are listed in Tables 4.1, 4.2, and 4.3. These morphemes are not meant for recitation or memorization in isolation. Rather, they

Table 4.1 Common Prefixes in Science Vocabulary[16]

a-/ab-	= away, not	en-	= in, to cause	ob-/oc-/of-/op-	= toward, against
ad-	= forward	equi-	= equal, same		
aero-	= air	ex-	= out, intensive	omni-	= all
amphi-	= both			ped-	= foot
ante-	= before	geo-	= earth	per-	= throughout
anti-	= against, opposite	heter-	= different	peri-	= around
		homo-	= same	photo-	= light
archae-	= ancient, chief	horti-	= garden	phono-	= sound
arthro-	= jointed	hydro-	= water	poly-	= more than one
audio-	= hearing, sound	hyper-	= over	pre-	= before
		hypo-	= below normal	primi-	= first, original
auto-	= self			pro-	= in favor of, before
bi-	= two	idio-	= individual		
bio-	= life	infra-	= beneath, inferior to	proto-	= earliest
cardio-	= heart			post-	= after, behind
chemo-	= chemical	inter	= between	quadri-	= four
chloro-	= green	intra-/intro-	= within	re-	= back, again
chroma-	= color	iso-	= equal, uniform	semi-	= half
circum-	= around, circle			spher-	= round
centi-	= one hundredth	mal-	= bad, abnormal	strato-	= horizontal layer
co-/col-/com-/con-	= together	meta-	= change, next	sub-	= under
contra-	= opposed			super-	= over
de-	= down	meter-/metr-	= measure	supra-	= beyond
di-	= two	meso-	= middle	tele-	= distant
dia-	= across, through	micro-	= small, one millionth	thermo-	= heat
dis-	= not, away, apart	milli-	= one thousandth	trans-	= across
				tri-	= three
dys-	= bad, difficult	mono-	= single	ultra-	= above, beyond
eco-	= environment	morph-	= form, shape		
ecto-/exo-/extra-	= outside	multi-	= many	un-	= not
		noct-	= night	uni-	= one
electro-	= electricity	non-	= not		

Table 4.2	Common Roots in Science Vocabulary[17]

bene	= well	**fract**	= to break	**spect/spic**	= to look
caten	= bind	**ject**	= to throw	**spir**	= to breathe
cred	= to believe	**med**	= middle	**still**	= to drip
derm	= skin	**mis/mit**	= to send	**struct**	= to build
dict	= to say	**pend**	= to hang	**tend**	= to stretch
duc	= to lead	**port**	= to carry	**tract**	= to pull or draw
fac/fact	= to make	**pos/pon**	= to place		
fer	= to carry	**press**	= to press	**ven/vent**	= to come
flect/flex	= to bend	**rupt**	= to break	**vers/vert**	= to turn
flu	= to flow	**scrib/script**	= to write	**vid/vis**	= to see
form	= to shape	**sect**	= to cut		

Table 4.3	Common Suffixes in Science Vocabulary[18]

-able/-ible	= capable of, worthy of, inclined to be	**-ism**	= action, characteristic behavior/quality, doctrine
-al	= action, relating to, characterized by	**-itis**	= disease of
-ance/-ence	= condition, state, action	**-ity**	= condition, quality
-ant/-ent	= performing/ promoting/causing a specified action	**-ive**	= performing or tending toward a specified action
		-ium	= chemical element or group
-ary	= pertaining to	**-ize**	= cause to be or become
-ate	= having, characterized by, to act upon in a specified manner	**-less**	= without
		-ly	= in the manner of
-cide	= killing	**-ment**	= action, process, means
-cy	= condition, action	**-ness**	= quality, condition
-cyte	= cell	**-ology**	= a branch of learning
-dom	= state, domain	**-osis**	= condition, disease
-er/-or	= one that is or performs a specified action	**-ous**	= full of, characterized by
		-pod	= foot
-ful	= full of	**-th**	= process, state, quality
-ian	= relating to, resembling, an expert of	**-tion/-sion**	= action, process
		-tious	= characterized by
-ic	= of, pertaining to, characterized by	**-ude**	= state, quality
		-ular	= of, relating to, resembling
-ine	= chemical	**-ward**	= in the direction of
-ion	= process, condition	**-y**	= characterized by, consisting of, tending toward, somewhat

can be introduced incrementally as they appear in key words that belong to a particular unit of study in science. They can be taught in conjunction with other aspects of vocabulary studies, such as scientific meaning versus everyday meaning, semantically related words versus orthographically similar words, synonyms, and antonyms. Effective morphemic analysis lessons are characterized by clear explanation, modeling, guided practices, and meaningful applications.

A cautionary note is in order here. Even though some vocabulary words may contain the spelling patterns identified here as prefix, root, or suffix, these spelling patterns may not be "morphemes" in those particular words. For example, in the word *refraction, re-* is a prefix meaning "back." However, *re-* is not a morpheme in words like *realism* and *reeve.* Helping students recognize whether a particular spelling pattern constitutes a morpheme is important in teaching morphemic analysis.

Table 4.4 lists a few of the technical words that are analyzed morphemically. These words were taken from a sixth-grade science textbook.

Table 4.4 Sample Science Vocabulary Words for Morphemic Analysis

Science Vocabulary	Morphemes	Word Meaning
Archaebacteria	archae + bacteria	The most primitive living single-celled organisms
Bioremediation	bio + re + medi + ate + ion	The use of biological means (such as adding bacteria) to clean up contaminated land
Chlorine	chlor + ine	A poisonous, corrosive, greenish-yellow chemical
Compressional	com + press + ion + al	Related to the reduction of the volume or mass of something
Decomposer	de + com + pos + er	An organism that causes organic matter to rot or decay
Distillation	dis + still + ate + ion	The process of separating, concentrating, or purifying
Fleshy	flesh + y	Having flesh
Isobar	iso + bar	A line on a map connecting points of equal pressure

(Continued)

Table 4.4   (Continued)

Science Vocabulary	Morphemes	Word Meaning
Omnivore	omni + vore	An animal that eats both animals and plants
Phytoremediation	phyto + re + medi + ate + ion	Using plants to help clean up soil
Pollutant	pollute + ant	Something that pollutes
Protostar	proto + star	The earliest star
Refraction	re + fract + ion	Changes in direction when a wave passes from one medium to another
Unappetizing	un + appetite + ize + ing	Having the quality of causing stomach not to have craving for something

Vocabulary Think Chart

Another strategy for developing students' knowledge about science vocabulary is to use a vocabulary think chart. The questions in this think chart (see Table 4.5) are designed to stimulate students' thinking and discussion about the target vocabulary word and to increase their conceptual understanding of the word.

Table 4.5   Vocabulary Think Chart[19]

Questions	Answers
What is the target word?	
Do you recognize any part of the word, such as prefix, suffix, or root (or base word)? What does each part mean?	
What does the word remind you of? Can you give a semantically related word, an orthographically similar word, or a real-life vignette triggered by the word?	

Questions	Answers
How is the word defined in the text? Can you paraphrase this definition?	
Can you come up with a sentence in which the target word is used in the scientific sense?	
This word is part of which larger science concept? What are some other words related to this larger concept?	

This vocabulary think chart can be completed as a group and/or an individual activity after the reading of text or at the conclusion of a unit of study to help students review key concepts related to the unit. For example, in a sixth-grade unit on waves, the think chart was used to help students understand and differentiate the key terms related to types of wave (*mechanical, electromagnetic, transverse, compressional, longitudinal*), properties of wave (*amplitude, wavelength, frequency, trough, crest*), and behaviors of wave (*reflection, refraction, diffraction, interference*). Using the think chart as a guide, Maria shared the following with her sixth-grade peers:

> My word is *refraction.* I know the word has three meaningful parts: *re-* means "back," *fract* means "break," and *-ion* means "process." This word reminds me of another word that looks similar: *reflection.* It also reminds me of something I observe everyday, that is, a spoon appears bent when standing in a glass of water. In science, this word means "breaking up light or sound waves." By that I mean the light or sound wave changes directions when it passes from one medium to another or through the same medium that has a different temperature and density. A sentence in which this word can be used is "Mirage is an interesting example of atmospheric refraction." The word is part of the larger concept called "behaviors of wave." Other words in the category include *reflection, refraction, diffraction,* and *interference.*

Concept Definition Word Map

One activity that teachers can use to enrich students' conceptual understanding of technical vocabulary following morphemic analysis or on its own is the concept definition word map, developed by

Robert Schwartz and Taffy Raphael.[20] A concept definition word map has three components: (1) what is it (probing category/classification), (2) what is it like/what does it do/what does it have (probing attributes), and (3) what are some examples (probing illustrations). These components are organized graphically in order to give students a visual representation of the meaning of the target word.

When using a concept definition word map, students can start by placing a key concept (like *arthropod*) in the center of a blank sheet of paper and then adding information under each of the three components (see Figure 4.1). This can be done as a before-reading activity to

Figure 4.1 Concept Definition Word Map for "Arthropod"

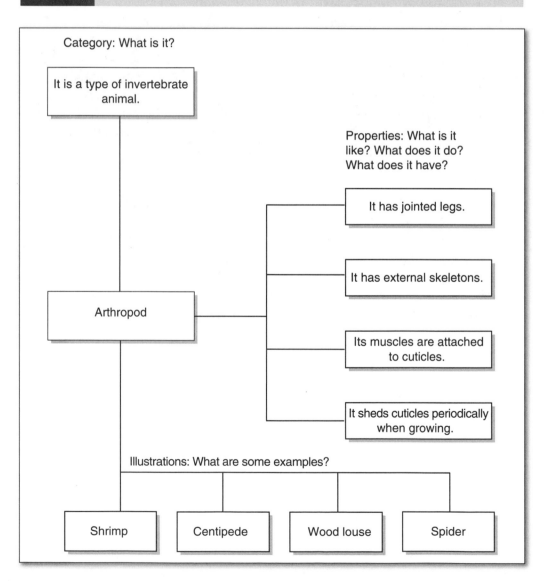

Category: What is it?

It is a type of invertebrate animal.

Properties: What is it like? What does it do? What does it have?

It has jointed legs.

It has external skeletons.

Arthropod

Its muscles are attached to cuticles.

It sheds cuticles periodically when growing.

Illustrations: What are some examples?

Shrimp | Centipede | Wood louse | Spider

activate or assess students' prior knowledge about the concept. It can also be done as a during- or after-reading activity to help students construct, consolidate, and demonstrate understanding of the concept. Students can then compare and contrast their word maps in small-group sharing or whole-class discussion.

Vocabulary Self Collection

Vocabulary self collection, or VSS, is an activity developed by Martha Haggard to promote ownership and learning of content vocabulary.[21] It engages students in collaboratively generating a list of words important to the content and discussing the meaning of these words. The activity encourages students to make connections between what they are learning and what they already know from prior experiences. It has the potential to stimulate students' fascination with the language of science and increase their enjoyment of the subject. The following four steps are involved in using the activity:

1. Reading and selecting words. In this stage, the class is divided into cooperative groups of two to five students. Each group reads the assigned text (textbook excerpt, trade book, and/or magazine/journal article), discusses it, and then chooses words they deem important to understanding the topic.

2. Defining, explaining, and illustrating the words. Members of each group work together to define, explain, and illustrate the words they have selected. They can use morphemic analysis, prior knowledge, glossaries (or dictionaries), and/or contextual clues to help them figure out the meanings of these words.

3. Finalizing the word lists. Each group nominates their words to the class, with an explanation of where the words are found in the text, why these words are important for the class to learn, what their meanings are, and how the meanings are determined. After all groups have submitted their VIP words, the class finalizes the vocabulary list by deleting duplicate words or words students already know. The final vocabulary list—with each word clearly defined, explained, and illustrated—can be displayed as a class poster and recorded in students' science journals or notebooks. The class can vote to award a small prize to the group(s) that has done the most amazing job selecting and presenting the words.

4. Extending word knowledge. The final vocabulary list can be referred to during the unit study, used as a spelling list, included as key words in writing assignments, or made a part of the unit assessment.

Word Sort

Word sort is another language-based activity that can be used to promote vocabulary growth in science and other content areas.[22] It helps students recognize common properties among core concepts. The activity can be used before a unit to gauge students' prior knowledge or after a unit to assess their learning. In word sort, students are given a list of words, identify the meaning and features of each word, and then sort the words into distinct categories, with words in each category sharing similar features. The steps below can be followed when implementing this activity:

1. Identify 12 to 20 key vocabulary words. These words are compiled by the teacher based on the reading selections and/or come from the vocabulary self-collection list that students have generated. Write each word on an index card.

2. Divide the class into small groups of three to five students. Give each group a complete set of index cards with the list of target words.

3. Have each group sort the words into predetermined categories provided by the teacher (called "close sort") or into the categories that the groups deem appropriate (called "open sort").

4. Have each group present their word list for each category and defend their sorting by explaining how they come up with the categories and how each word in the category meets the specified criteria.

For example, words like *annelids, cambium, cnidarians, crocodiles, ferns, horsetails, liverworts, lizards, mosses, marsupials, monotremes, phloem, sponges,* and *xylem* can be sorted into two close categories of plants (*cambium, ferns, horsetails, liverworts, mosses, phloem, xylem*) and animals (*annelids, cnidarians, crocodiles, lizards, marsupials, monotremes, sponges*). They can also be open sorted into the categories of, for instance, seedless nonvascular plants (*liverworts, mosses*), seedless vascular plants (*horsetails, ferns*), plant vascular tissue (*xylem, phloem, cambium*), invertebrates (*annelids, cnidarians, sponges*), and vertebrates (*crocodiles, lizards, marsupials, monotremes*). Teachers can decide whether to use an open or a close sort based on the nature of the vocabulary list, the goal of the lesson, and students' grade level.

LEARNING ABOUT NOUNS

We have shown through the comparison of the Arthur text and the plant text in Chapter 2 that nouns—including technical nouns, abstract nouns, and long nouns—are a potential source of reading difficulty in science. Therefore, it is important that some tasks be designed to help students develop an understanding of the structures and functions of these nouns. Five such tasks are noun deconstruction, noun expansion, noun search, definition game, and sentence completion.

Noun Deconstruction

One way to help students tackle long, complex nouns is to analyze their structure. Structural analysis of this sort can further students' understanding of how information is typically packed and expanded in the language of science. A long noun in science consists of premodifiers, the head, and postmodifiers. For example, the underlined portion of this sentence from a science trade book, "The various species that survive in the depths of the ocean are rarely more than 12 inches (50 cm) long,"[23] is a long noun that contains two premodifiers (*the, various*), one head (*species*), and a postmodifier (*that survive in the depth of the ocean*). Premodifiers can include one or more of the following elements:

- Pointer, which is realized through articles (*a, the*), demonstrative pronouns (*this, those*), and possessive pronouns (*their, his*)
- Numerative, which is realized through numerals (*one, five*) and ordinals (*first, third*)
- Describer, which is realized through nongradable, intensifying adjectives (*definite, most, certain, absolute, extreme, entire, perfect, various*) and gradable adjectives (*important, lush, green*)
- Classifier, which is realized through adjectives with a proper noun basis denoting nationality, provenance, and style (*Australian mammal*); adjectives with a relation to nouns meaning "relating to" or "consisting of" (*medical, social, rural, annual, economic*); and nouns (*death* in the phrase *death rate* or *plant* in the phrase *plant growth*).

Postmodifiers, also called qualifiers, are typically realized through the following grammatical elements:

- Prepositional phrases (*of the ocean*)
- Embedded clauses (species *that survive in the depths of the ocean;* the land [that is] *to be reclaimed*)

The long noun (underlined) in the sentence, "<u>The familiar sequence of saddening events that begins with logging and ends with expensive deforestation of entire countries</u> is repeated in the Philippines,"[24] can be deconstructed as follows:

the	Premodifier: Pointer
familiar	Premodifier: Describer
sequence	Head
of saddening events	Postmodifier: Prepositional Phrase
that begins with logging and ends with the extensive deforestation of entire countries	Postmodifier: Embedded Clause

This example shows that the embedded clause is a key grammatical resource for packing a large amount of information into the nominal structure. Figure 4.2 further illustrates the power of noun deconstruction in revealing multiple layers of embedding in this sentence (with the long noun underlined) from a textbook passage reporting about the first documented air pollution disaster in the United States that occurred during October of 1948 in the town of Donora near Pittsburgh, Pennsylvania.

This killer fog resulted from <u>a combination of mountainous terrain surrounding the valley and weather conditions that trapped and concentrated deadly pollutants emitted by the community's steel mill, zinc smelter, and sulfur acid plant.</u>[25]

Figure 4.2   Noun Deconstruction

a	Premodifier: Pointer
combination	Head
of mountainous terrain surrounding the valley and weather conditions	Postmodifier: Prepositional Phrase
that trapped and concentrated deadly pollutants emitted by the community's steel mill, zinc smelter, and sulfur acid plant	Postmodifier: Embedded Clause

The prepositional phrase and the embedded clause in Figure 4.2 each contain an embedded clause (*surrounding the valley; emitted by the community's steel mill, zinc smelter, and sulfur acid plant*) that modifies "mountainous terrain" and "deadly pollutants," respectively.

Noun Expansion

Conversely, students can engage in what many teachers would call an "elaboration" task, which requires expanding simple nouns (*disaster*) into long nouns with pre- or postmodifiers (*the worst natural disaster in Florida that uprooted over 2 million people*). Figure 4.3 shows this expansion process.

Figure 4.3	Noun Expansion
Head:	disaster
Add Premodifier: Pointer	the disaster
Add Premodifier: Describer	the worst disaster
Add Premodifier: Classifier	the worst natural disaster
Add Postmodifier: Prepositional Phrase:	the worst natural disaster in Florida
Add Postmodifier: Embedded Clause:	the worst natural disaster in Florida that uprooted over 2 million people

Teachers can start out by having students add one or two modifiers to a simple noun and gradually increase the number of modifiers to be added as students gain more confidence in the task. Len Unsworth[26] suggests that the activity can be made into a game by having one student (Student A) nominate a pre- or postmodifier category and another student (Student B) then comes up with the appropriate word, phrase, or clause that instantiates that category. If Student B answers correctly, she scores one point and gets to nominate the next category of modifiers. If Students B answers incorrectly, he is out of the game. Students enjoy turning this game into a "building noun train" contest to see which student (or group of students) makes the longest "noun train" by adding as many pre- and postmodifiers as possible to a head.

Noun Search

Teachers can also have students identify nouns in the texts they have read or written, and list them as simple, long, technical, or abstract.[27] Simple nouns are defined here as pronouns (*this*), proper nouns (*New York, Charles Darwin*), or concrete nouns with no more than two premodifiers (*tigers, these mammals, the rain forest*). These categories of nouns may overlap because some nouns (*experimental verification of Einstein's explanation of the photoelectric effect*) are simultaneously technical, abstract, and lengthy.

We can look, for example, at the nouns used in the following excerpt from the plants issue of *Kids Discover:*

> Water that evaporates from the leaves of rain forest plants helps clouds form. Clouds bring rain. As the rain forest is reduced, the climate becomes drier. Scientists believe that the destruction of the rain forests in Africa has led to droughts and crop failures.[28]

We can identify nouns in this excerpt that are simple, long, abstract, and technical as follows:

Simple nouns:	clouds, rain, the rain forest, scientists
Long nouns:	water that evaporates from the leaves of rain forest plants, the destruction of the rain forests in Africa
Abstract nouns:	destruction, droughts, crop failures
Technical nouns:	evaporates, the climate

It is clear from this search that even at a young age, children are expected to deal with nouns that are technical, abstract, and long. Because of these nouns, some sentences in the excerpt, such as the last one, may be challenging for children to comprehend.

Another way to develop students' appreciation of how nouns are characteristically deployed in scientific texts is to have them compare the nouns used in the books they read with the nouns used in their own writing of like genres and topics. Students can also compare the nouns used in different genres (like stories in newspapers or reports in academic journals). Such comparison will sensitize students to the ways nouns are typically used by experts to present information and construct knowledge in particular content areas and genres. This should, in turn, help students become better readers and writers of science.

Table 4.6 displays two texts, a report about fish from a sixth-grade science textbook[29] and a text of the same genre on crocodiles by a seventh-grade student, who was asked to assume the role of a scientist-author and write an informational report on an animal with which she was most familiar.

Table 4.6	Comparison of Science Textbook Excerpt and Student Writing Sample

Textbook Excerpt (129 words)	Sample Student Text (142 words)
Fish are ectotherms that live in water and use gills to get oxygen. Gills are fleshy filaments that are filled with tiny blood vessels. The heart of the fish pumps blood to the gills. As blood passes through the gills, it picks up oxygen from water that is passing over the gills. Carbon dioxide is released from blood into the water. Most fish have fins. Fins are fanlike structures used for steering, balancing, and moving. Usually, they are paired. Those on the top and bottom stabilize the fish. Those on the side steer and move the fish. Scales are another common characteristic of fish, although not all fish have scales. Scales are hard, thin, overlapping plates that cover the skin. These protective plates are made of a bony material.	Crocodiles live in water but can walk on land. They are reptiles. Crocodiles have their noses right on top of their mouths, so when they are in water they can still breath. Crocodiles have scales and they are carnivores, which means they eat meat. Their teeth can bite through just about anything. Some crocodiles live in groups and some just live in a cave alone. Crocodiles eat birds, fish, and other types of meat. Because of their strong jaws they can bite through almost anything. Crocodiles can be scary and dangerous, so you should not go near them because they might bite you. Crocodile babies come from eggs and their mothers are very defensive if you get near them. Crocodiles are usually found in swamps. Some crocodiles live on land but their nests are usually in caves where the water flows in.
Simple nouns (23)	**Simple nouns (44)**
fish, gills, blood, the gills, blood, the gills, it, oxygen, carbon dioxide, blood, the water, most fish, fins, fins, they, the fish, the fish, scales, all fish, scales, scales, these protective plates, a bony material	crocodiles, water, land, they, reptiles, crocodiles, their noses, they, water, they, crocodiles, scales, they, carnivores, which, they, meat, their teeth, anything, some crocodiles, groups, some, a cave, crocodiles, birds, fish, their strong jaws, they, anything, crocodiles, you, them, they, you, crocodile babies, eggs, their mothers, you, them, crocodiles, swamps, some crocodiles, land, their nests
Long Nouns (9)	**Long Nouns (3)**
• ectotherms that live in water and use gills to get oxygen • fleshy filaments that are filled with tiny blood vessels	• top of the mouth • other types of meat • caves where the water flows in

(Continued)

Table 4.6	(Continued)

Textbook Excerpt (129 words)	Sample Student Text (142 words)
• the heart of the fish • water that is passing over the gills • fanlike structures used for steering, balancing, and moving • those on the top and bottom • those on the side • another common characteristic of fish • hard, thin, overlapping plates that cover the skin	
Technical Nouns (10) ectotherms, gills, oxygen, filaments, fins, vessels, characteristic, plates, carbon dioxide, scales	**Technical Nouns (2)** reptiles, carnivores

*Misspellings in the student text have been corrected for ease of reading.

A comparison of the two texts shows distinct patterns of noun use. The fish text contains a total of 32 nouns, 23 (72%) of which are simple and 9 (28%) long. The crocodile text, on the other hand, uses 47 nouns, 44 (94%) of which are simple and 3 (6%) long. Moreover, the fish text uses 10 different technical nouns, compared to 2 in the crocodile text. It is clear that the more "scientific" text tends to use longer and more complex nouns, whereas the more "everyday" text tends to use shorter and simpler nouns.

Definition Game

Definition is a key tool used by scientists to classify, define, and catalogue the natural world.[30] In defining technical concepts, long nouns are often used. The following examples (with long nouns italicized) are typical of what can be found in science textbooks and trade books:

- The cuticle is *a waxy, protective layer secreted by the cell wall.*[31]
- The cell membrane is *a structure that forms the outer boundary of the cell and allows only certain materials to move into and out of the cell.*[32]

- This [multichannel pipette] is *a series of droppers arranged in a line that adds tiny drops containing DNA into the wells of a tray ready for the sequencing process.*[33]
- A lightning bolt is *a giant spark of electric charge jumping from a thunder-cloud to the ground.*[34]
- A DNA registry is *a database that would genetically identify all whales taken for commercial or scientific purposes and make that information available to a monitoring body.*[35]
- Sandstone caves are *shallow, hollowed-out cavities in the base of cliffs made of a soft rock called sandstone.*[36]

A language-based task for teaching science-specific technical nouns is a definition game, to be played in small groups of three to five students.[37] In this game, the teacher prepares three decks of cards. In one deck are cards that have key technical terms from a current unit of study or units under review. These cards are called vocabulary cards. The second deck consists of cards that name the different categories of the nominal structure, that is, pointer, numerative, describer, classifier, head, and qualifier (that is, postmodifier). These cards are called category cards. They are written in capital letters, with one category per card. In the third deck, textbook or dictionary definitions of target technical nouns are written, and each definition is cut up so that each constituent of the definition is put on one card. These are called definition cards. For example, the definition of "gigantoraptor"—*a giant, birdlike dinosaur that is as tall as the formidable tyrannosaur*—is cut up into five cards (*a, giant, birdlike, dinosaur, that is as tall as the formidable tyrannosaur*), each representing a constituent of the nominal structure (pointer, describer, classifier, head, qualifier).

At the start of the game, the vocabulary cards (three to five cards at a time) are placed face up at the lower left side of the table. The category cards are shuffled and placed face down in the middle of the table. The cut-up definition cards are also shuffled and placed face up in the upper right side of the table. Each player must take a category card from the middle of the table and then look for a corresponding definition card in the upper right side of the table to be put next to the appropriate vocabulary card in the lower left side of the table. For example, if a player picks "HEAD" from the deck of category cards, he must then find a corresponding definition card, such as "dinosaur," which is then to be placed next to the vocabulary card "gigantoraptor." Each correct placement scores one point. The teacher or an experienced student can monitor the game by being a referee. This game can help students consolidate their knowledge of the nominal structure. It gives them a chance to play with technical grammar of science while also learning science content.

Sentence Completion

As Chapter 2 demonstrates, nominalizations are often used to synthesize a chunk of prior text in order to create new technical terms or virtual entities for further discussion and to facilitate the flow of information presentation. Teachers can design tasks that highlight this aspect of scientific language. One such task is sentence completion.[38] Sentence completion requires students to synthesize information in the previous sentence(s) into a noun that can then become the subject, or point of departure, for discussion in the next sentence. Teachers can identify passages in science textbooks or trade books that contain nominalizations and take out the nominalizations for students to fill in, as the following examples show:

- To reduce air pollution, many people keep their cars well tuned. _____ use gas more efficiently and produce fewer pollutants.[39] [sample key: Well-tuned cars]
- Cocoa cultivation spread so rapidly around the tropics that all the cultivated trees were developed from a very few wild ancestors. _____ made modern cultivated varieties vulnerable to disease.[40] [sample key: This lack of genetic variation]
- Prior to the 1960s a number of drugs, such as Atabrine and chloroquine, had been developed that effectively treated this illness [malaria]. Unfortunately, patients would often use only enough of these medicines to reduce the symptoms, saving the rest for future bouts of the disease. Many of the microscopic parasites that produced malaria would survive _____ (1) and produce offspring capable of withstanding a full dose of the medicine. _____ (2) began to appear among U.S. troops during the Vietnam War, in which more soldiers were incapacitated by the disease than by battle wounds. Despite _____ (3) of different, more powerful drug, the new kind of malaria spread across Asia, then to Africa, and eventually to South America.[41] [sample keys: (1) the sublethal dose; (2) This drug-resistant type of malaria; (3) the introduction]

As a variation, the more everyday form of a nominalization can be used as a clue and students are to replace the clue with a nominalization that makes it sound more abstract and scientific, as this example from Chapter 2 illustrates:

- Plate tectonics is one process that causes changing environments on Earth. As plates on Earth's surface moved over time, continents collided with and separated from each other many times. Continental collisions caused _____ (1) and _____ (2). _____ (3) caused deeper seas to develop between continents. _____ (4) still causes changes in climates today. [sample keys: (1) mountain building, (2) the draining of seas, (3) Continental separation, (4) This rearrangement of land and sea]

Sentence completion tasks such as these can help students see how nominalization allows the text writer to summarize or synthesize a wide range of grammatical and semantic data that have been previously presented in the text into an abstract or virtual entity so that it can be used as the subject for further discussion. Such exercises allow students to gain insights into the development of cohesive texts that flow. They also make students better able to figure out the meaning of the abstract or technical terms that derive from the grammatical process of nominalization.

DISENTANGLING DISCOURSE

Finally, we describe three language-based tasks that are designed to help students unpack and display the organization and logic of the language of science at the discourse level. These are developing awareness of textual signposts, syntactic anatomy and integration, and paraphrasing.

Developing Awareness of Textual Signposts

Science is a discipline that relies not only on hands-on experiences but also the logic of argument.[42] Scientists are trained to be both accurate and precise in conducting scientific activities; they are careful about their use of language when offering explanations, describing phenomena, discussing theories, and making claims. Scientists need to make coherent and organized arguments in order to avoid inconsistencies and contradictions and to convince the scientific community of their theories. In constructing such rhetorical arguments, they use not only connectives (such as conjunctions) but other grammatical devices (such as nouns, verbs, and prepositional phrases) to signal logical reasoning.

We noted in Chapter 2 the importance of recognizing logical metaphors in science reading. Understanding how connectives such as conjunctions are used by scientists is also important in understanding scientific reasoning. For example, conjunctions are used in different ways across different contexts: In everyday language, a few common conjunctions (*and, and then, but, so, because, if*) are used, often in vague and imprecise ways; this is contrary to science, which uses a varied set of conjunctions with restricted, precise meanings.[43] Figure 4.4 identifies some of the commonly used connectives in science texts.

Figure 4.4	Common Connectives Used in Science Texts[44]
Addition:	and, in addition to, moreover, furthermore, also, nor
Contrast:	but, on the other hand, yet, however, conversely, whereas
Elaboration:	that is, in other words, for instance, for example, to illustrate
Causation:	therefore, hence, as a result, for this reason, because
Comparison:	likewise, unlike, similarly, in contrast, as
Concession:	yet, still, nevertheless, while, though, despite that
Conditional:	otherwise, when, if, unless
Sequential:	finally, previously, next, secondly, lastly, meanwhile, as, while, when
Summation:	in short, in conclusion, to sum up
Choice:	whether, instead

These connectives link sentences and paragraphs in a text in many different ways, including clarifying (*in other words, that is, to illustrate*), indicating time (*previously, at the same time, until then*), adding information (*furthermore, as well, along with*), showing cause and effect (*therefore, accordingly, as a result*), sequencing ideas (*first, in conclusion, to begin*), stating condition or concession (*however, on the other hand, on the contrary*), and providing comparison and contrast (*on the other hand, similarly, whereas, conversely*). However, they are often taken for granted or misunderstood in science reading.[45] To understand the logic of science, it is important that students pay attention to the connectives that can cue them in to what has been said earlier in the text and what is to come next. To enhance students' awareness

> *To understand the logic of science, it is important that students pay attention to the connectives that can cue them in to what has been said earlier in the text and what is to come next.*

and understanding of these textual signposts, teachers can construct sentence completion exercises that require students to supply the deleted or missing connectives. They can also draw students' attention to—and discuss the meanings of—textual connectives during read alouds or individual conferences. These exercises will increase students' understanding of scientific reasoning and develop their ability to make logical, coherent arguments in science.

Syntactic Anatomy and Integration

Unlike the chaining syntax of everyday language, where clauses are often strung together through coordination (*and, and then, so*) and subordination (*if, when, as, after, because*), scientific language employs complex sentences with hierarchical structure using both subordinate clauses and embedded clauses. These types of sentences are needed in science because they enable scientists to more accurately and effectively present information and make logical arguments. However, comprehension problems can arise when a sentence comprises multiple clauses where layers of semantic links and dependency relationships take time for students to sort through. An overemphasis on fluency in reading these texts can be detrimental to comprehension.

Let's consider the following excerpt (with underlining added) from a science trade book:

It had already been known <u>that</u> DNA was the molecule of <u>which</u> genes are made <u>when</u> two young scientists, James Watson and Francis Crick, took on the challenge of figuring out its structure. In 1953 they constructed a model <u>that</u> showed <u>that</u> each DNA molecule consisted of two long chains <u>that</u> spiraled around each other in a twisted ladder shape—a double helix.[46]

The first sentence of this excerpt consists of two subordinate clauses, the first introduced by "that" (*that DNA was the molecule of which genes are made*) and the second by "when" (*when two young scientists, James Watson and Francis Crick, took on the challenge of figuring out its structure*). Nested in the first subordinate clause is an embedded clause (*of which genes are made*).

In the second sentence, the first "that" introduces an embedded clause to modify "a model" (*that showed . . .*). Within this embedded clause, the second "that" introduces a subordinate clause following the verb "showed" (*that each DNA molecule consisted of two long chains*). Within this subordinate clause, an embedded clause introduced by the third "that" is used to modify the noun "two long chains" (*that spiraled around each other in a twisted ladder shape—a double helix*). Readers will have to be able to process these multiple layers of embedding as well as logical and dependency relationships within a reasonable timeframe in order to ensure successful comprehension.

Students need help sorting out these complex sentence structures. Teachers can engage students in analyzing and discussing the different ways clauses are combined to form complex sentences and make meaning in science. After the analysis and discussion, students rewrite the target sentences in their own language to clarify understanding. As a variation, teachers can have one student (or group of students) deconstruct a complex sentence and rewrite it using the more "fragmented" syntax of spoken language. Another student (or group of students) is to put the "fragmented" sentences back into the more in integrated, scientific mode.

For example, the following sentence (with underlining added) from a seventh-grade science textbook is made up of one main clause (*Bacteria live along portions of the mid-ocean ridges*), two subordinate clauses (*where superheated water either seeps or blasts from the crust; as shown in Figure 14–7*), and one embedded clause (*that perform chemosynthesis using sulfur compounds*). Together, these four clauses construct a complex sentence that describes the activities of bacteria.

> *Bacteria <u>that</u> perform chemosynthesis using sulfur compounds live along portions of the mid-ocean ridges, <u>where</u> superheated water either seeps or blasts from the crust, <u>as</u> shown in Figure 14–7.*[47]

Having deconstructed the complex sentence into several clauses, students can then rewrite the sentence as: *Bacteria use sulfur compounds to perform chemosynthesis. Bacteria live along portions of the mid-ocean ridges. In the mid-ocean ridges, superheated water either seeps or blasts from the crust. This is shown in Figure 14–7.* At another time or with another group of students, the teacher can have students practice integrating these simpler sentences into a more complex sentence.

Similarly, students can deconstruct and reconstruct long, complex science definitions. For instance, one student can break this definition— *A tornado is a violently rotating column of air that reaches from the clouds to the ground*—into several sentences, such as *"A tornado is a column of air. The air reaches from the clouds to the ground, and it rotates violently."* Another student then puts these sentences back into one sentence to form a scientific definition of tornado.

Syntactic anatomy and integration of the sort described here enables students to move back and forth between the more familiar and the more alien patterns of language, helping them better construct scientific definitions and cope with the challenging syntax of science texts. Research has suggested the usefulness of such exercises in improving students' comprehension and composition of academic texts.[48]

Paraphrasing

As we have demonstrated in Chapter 2, the language of science can be simultaneously technical, dense, abstract, metaphorical, impersonal, and authoritative. One coping strategy is to have students learn to disentangle, or unpack, the language of school science by translating the patterns of written language in science into everyday spoken language. Jay Lemke has suggested that it is through the more familiar and comfortable language of everyday speech that students reason themselves through problems to arrive at understanding.[49]

> One coping strategy is to have students learn to disentangle, or unpack, the language of school science by translating the patterns of written language in science into everyday spoken language.

A classroom activity that promotes paraphrasing practice is to have students, individually or in small groups of two to three, develop a pop science radio show series.[50] In this activity, students are invited to contribute scripts for a school radio show aimed at popularizing science. Students are given a written informational text on a topic they have been studying in science. They are to read the written text and then turn a section (or all) of the text into a spoken script suitable to be taped for a radio show. After taping, students listen to the tape and prepare to discuss what they did to the written text to make it into more speechlike forms. The teacher can put the original written text and the spoken script from students on an overhead to highlight the grammatical differences between the original and the paraphrased versions. This activity helps students develop a better awareness of and insights into the differences between scientific ways of using language and everyday ways of using language. To improve students' paraphrasing skills, the teacher can conduct minilessons on how to unpack nominalizations, long nouns, and logical metaphors into more congruent forms of everyday language.

Table 4.7 presents a written explanation about the rise of infectious bacteria excerpted from a school science textbook[51] and its paraphrased version constructed by a group of eighth-grade students.

Table 4.7	Written and Paraphrased (Spoken) Versions of Science Explanation	

Written	Spoken
The incredible genetic adaptability of bacteria is one reason the world faces a potentially serious rise in the incidence of some infectious bacteria diseases once controlled by antibiotics. Other factors also play a role, including (1) spread of bacteria (some beneficial and some harmful) around the globe by human travel and the trade of goods, (2) overuse of antibiotics by doctors, often at the insistence of their patients (with a 2000 study by Richard Wenzel and Michael Edward suggesting that at least half of all antibiotics used to treat humans are prescribed unnecessarily), (3) failure of many patients to take all of their prescribed antibiotics, which promotes bacterial resistance, (4) availability of antibiotics in many countries without prescriptions, (5) overuse of pesticides, which increases populations of pesticide-resistant insects and other carriers of bacterial diseases, and (6) widespread use of antibiotics in the livestock and dairy industries to control disease in livestock animals and to promote animal growth.	Because bacteria genes are incredibly adaptable, there may be many more cases of infectious bacteria diseases in the world. Some of these bacteria diseases used to be controlled by antibiotics. Other factors also play a role. First, bacteria, good or bad, are spread around the globe because people travel and goods are traded from one place to another. Second, doctors use antibiotics too much mostly because their patients insist on using them. For example, Richard Wenzel and Michael Edward conducted a study in 2000 and found that at least half of all antibiotics used to treat humans are unnecessarily prescribed. Third, many patients do not take all of their prescribed antibiotics. This makes bacteria more resistant to antibiotics. Fourth, in many countries people can get antibiotics without a prescription from their doctor. Fifth, humans use too much pesticide. Because of this, there are now more insects that are resistant to pesticides and more other carriers of bacteria diseases. Sixth, the livestock and dairy industries use antibiotics widely to make animals healthier and grow more quickly.

Some of the linguistic differences between the two versions are highlighted below:

Original (Written) Version	Paraphrased (Spoken) Version
• the incredible genetic adaptability of bacteria	• bacteria genes are incredibly adaptable
• one reason	• because
• potentially serious rise	• there may be many more cases
• spread of bacteria	• bacteria are spread
• human travel	• people travel
• the trade of goods	• goods are traded
• overuse of antibiotics by doctors	• doctors use antibiotics too much
• with a 2000 study by Richard Wenzel and Michael Edward	• For example, Richard Wenzel and Michael Richard conducted a study in 2000
• failure of many patients to take . . .	• many patients do not take . . .

It is clear from this comparison that much of the paraphrasing involves unpacking abstract nouns (nominalizations), long nouns, and metaphorical realizations of logical reasoning into grammatical forms more congruent with everyday uses of language. These grammatical differences between the written and spoken versions can be highlighted for class discussion.

Unlike the language of science, which focuses on things and their relations, the language of everyday life tends to foreground action and agents.[52] During paraphrasing, teachers can point out the similarities and differences between the written language of science and the spoken language of everyday life, highlighting aspects of daily life that can not be readily refined or distilled as well as those in the science domain that are not readily translatable into everyday language. Such exercises can help "avoid simplistic transfers of ways of thinking from everyday life into science, or vice versa."[53] Understanding scientific ways with words is critical to students' learning of the forms and functions of scientific language and to their development of communicative competence in science.

CONCLUSION

In a recent article in the *International Journal of Science Education*, science educators Larry Yore and David Treagust lamented a lack of theoretical base or empirical evidence in many of the language-based activities recommended for science teachers. They wrote,

> An informal survey of language in science teaching articles in teacher journals (*Instructor, Reading Teacher, Science Teacher, Science and Children, Science Scope, Science Activities,* and others) indicates numerous suggested applications for classroom practice with little or no theoretical or evidential base to justify their claims. Most of these professional articles are based on "craft" experience and personal opinions.[54]

The language-based tasks described in this chapter address the legitimate concern raised by Yore and Treagust. They have a theoretical base in sociolinguistics[55] and have been found to be effective in helping students cope with the language demands of content-area reading and writing.[56] According to Veel and Coffin,

> There is now considerable evidence as to the viability and successful outcomes of explicit teaching about the specialised language of schooling [such as the language of school science]. This includes substantial anecdotal evidence from teachers and students as well as more empirically based work by researchers and evaluators.[57]

The tasks recommended in this chapter do not always have to be carried out as isolated worksheet practices. They can be used with connected texts in authentic reading and writing and as a part of reading and writing workshops in the context of inquiry science. Their focus should be to develop students' linguistic awareness and insights, not to impart linguistic rules for memorization and recitation. These linguistically informed activities can complement and extend the reading strategies that are recommended in major content area reading textbooks[58] and professional development materials.[59]

Given the peculiar nature of scientific language and the developmental needs of students, explicit teaching should be carried out in a manner featuring a gradual release of responsibility. Specifically, there should be a great deal of teacher modeling in the beginning. As students gain more experience and confidence, they can then engage in collaborative work, initially with the teacher and subsequently with their peers, to explore the specialized language of school science, before eventually moving to independent practices. By explicitly addressing the linguistic challenges of school science, teachers help break down the barriers between the learner and the text and are in a better position to promote science literacy for all students.

5

Scaffolding Reading Through Strategy Instruction

We have suggested that understanding scientific ways of using language is a key component of science literacy. We have also described language-based tasks for developing students' knowledge about and insight into the specialized language of science. In this chapter, our focus is on using reading strategies to scaffold students' interaction with science texts. Specifically, we describe nine reading strategies that help students activate and integrate prior knowledge, regulate their own reading processes, and organize the information they learn from text. Some of these strategies are teacher initiated and content focused, whereas other strategies are student directed and are intended to promote independence in reading and studying.[1] Regardless of their orientations, these strategies all aim at promoting the use of cognitive and metacognitive skills (such as predicting, inferencing, monitoring, visualizing, questioning) that students have typically acquired by the time they begin formal schooling but often fail to activate and employ due to a lack of relevant background knowledge and/or language proficiencies.[2] They can be used not only in science, but in other content areas as well. Finally, we discuss guiding principles for reading strategy instruction in the science classroom and share sample science lesson plans that illustrate these principles.

READING STRATEGY INSTRUCTION AND TEXT COMPREHENSION

Reading is a complex process involving the use of strategies for integrating prior knowledge, monitoring comprehension, and retaining text information. Many students often do not spontaneously use these strategies in their reading. For example, reading psychologist Michael Pressley reported that there is little evidence of students "attacking a text on a first reading using the complex repertoire of strategies that are used by skilled readers."[3] This suggests that students need explicit instruction on how to use a repertoire of reading strategies to help them more effectively activate and integrate prior knowledge, detect breakdowns in comprehension, and organize and retain text information. This need becomes even more pronounced when students read the often technical, dense, and abstract texts of science. As Wellington and Osborne have noted, "Learning to read science from any source requires structured and scaffolded interaction with text."[4]

Several prominent reviews of research have identified strategy instruction as a critical component of successful literacy programs.[5] They confirmed that teaching an array of reading strategies can enhance students' understanding of the often abstract and complex texts in academic content areas. Skilled readers possess a flexible repertoire of strategies that they purposefully and effectively apply before, during, and after reading. According to Brown, Pressley, van Meter, and Schuder, skilled readers "are planful and goal-oriented when they read, combine their background knowledge with text cues to create meaning, apply a variety of strategies (e.g., from seeking the important information in text to noting details), monitor their comprehension, attempt to solve their comprehension problems, and evaluate their understanding and performance."[6] Teaching students how to behave like skilled readers can improve their comprehension and learning.[7] Numerous studies have demonstrated that explicit teaching of reading strategies in the science classroom improves students' understanding of science concepts and promotes development of science literacy.[8] In this chapter, we describe three types of strategies that have been documented to facilitate learning from the expository texts in content areas like science. These include

1. strategies that activate and develop prior knowledge,

2. strategies that promote comprehension monitoring, and

3. strategies that encourage organization of text information for recall and review.

READING STRATEGY INSTRUCTION IN ACTION: A VIGNETTE

Mrs. Fugate's sixth-grade science class had just begun a unit on measurement and was to learn about measuring temperature. Mrs. Fugate introduced a new reading strategy called "Questioning: Thick and Thin Questions."[9] She explained

> A thick question deals with the big picture or large concepts. It's one that often leads to deeper discussion and requires you to look beyond the text to find the answer. The answer to a thick question is often long and involved. You might have to do further research because the answer may not be right there in the text. A thick question often begins with '"Why?" "How come?" or "I wonder." A thin question can usually be answered with a simple "yes" or "no." The answer to a thin question may be right there in the text. A thin question is asked to clarify information, figure out the meaning of a new word, or make sense of a confusing section of the text.

Mrs. Fugate went on to tell her students that the reason people ask questions about what they read is to help them think about and make sense of what they are reading. She then read aloud an excerpt from a trade book titled *Temperature: Understanding Science*[10] and directed her students to follow along in their copies and think of their own questions as she read. She wrote some of her thick and thin questions on the overhead projector to model what they might look like. She continued to read aloud but this time directed her students to write one "thick question" on the big sticky note and one "thin question" on the small sticky note. (Both large and small sticky notes had been handed out at the beginning of the lesson.) She stopped reading and asked the students to share some of their questions. "Why is mercury silver?" asked one student. "How does the liquid cool off?" inquired another. The teacher told her students to continue reading the excerpt on their own and make note of any additional thick or thin questions they thought of as they read. After reading, the students were so eager to share their questions with the class that the teacher asked them to pair up and share their thick and thin questions with each other.

At the end of the lesson, Mrs. Fugate collected the sticky notes and later compiled the students' questions into a chart (see Table 5.1).

Table 5.1	Thick and Thin Questions About Measuring Temperature

Thin Questions	Thick Questions
• Who is Gabriel Fahrenheit? • When was the thermometer invented? • Where does the name Celsius come from? • How does the liquid cool off? • What is Celsius? • Who invented the Kelvin scale? • What is the difference between Celsius and Fahrenheit? • What is a physicist? • What kind of tube did they fill with alcohol and mercury? • What temperature does water boil at? • What is a meteorologist? • What does "designated" mean? • Why does the liquid in the thermometer expand? • Can you make a thermometer for below 0 degrees? • How do meteorologists check the weather? • Was Galileo Galilei given a Nobel Prize? • Why is the liquid in the thermometer red? • Did Fahrenheit test this more than once?	• Why is the measurement inconsistent when the temperature is taken in the sun? • I wonder why the temperature changes how much room the liquid takes up? • Why does water boil at 212 degrees and freeze at 32 degrees? • Why isn't Celsius used in the U.S.A.? • Why would Anders Celsius make the Celsius scale when he already had Fahrenheit? • Why do we have different scales for temperature measurement? • Is there a difference between using alcohol and mercury to measure temperature? • Why is mercury silver? • How does a metal (mercury) stay in liquid form at room temperature? • I wonder where the mercury rock is found. • Why did the scientists invent these thermometers? • Why do liquids expand more than solids?

She used the chart to discover her students' science misconceptions and to design instruction that responded to students' interests and curiosities. Subsequent class activities within the measurement unit were guided by the questions in this chart.

This vignette illustrates what can happen when reading strategy instruction is infused into the science lesson. Using strategies such as thick and thin questions helps students relate prior knowledge to text, stimulates their engagement

Using strategies such as thick and thin questions helps students relate prior knowledge to text, stimulates their engagement with the reading task, encourages monitoring of the comprehension process, and promotes inquiry and active learning of content.

with the reading task, encourages monitoring of the comprehension process, and promotes inquiry and active learning of content. In the rest of the chapter, we describe nine strategies that teachers can use to help their students activate and integrate prior knowledge, regulate their reading processes, and organize text information for further review and study.

BOOTSTRAPPING COMPREHENSION: ACTIVATING AND INTEGRATING PRIOR KNOWLEDGE

Prior knowledge, or schema, is perhaps the most important building block of any comprehension.[11] As such, it should be a focal piece of comprehension instruction. We describe three strategies that have been found useful in the science classroom. They are anticipation guide, K-W-L, and prior knowledge monitoring and integrating (PKMI).

Anticipation Guide

An anticipation guide is a tool to get students to think about the content of the text before reading begins.[12] The teacher presents a series of statements about the content of the text to students. The statements allow the teacher to identify students' misconceptions about science and to plan instruction. Students read and think about the statements before reading begins. During reading, they check to see if their opinions about the statements are supported or refuted in the text. After reading, students return to the anticipation guide and compare their understanding of the text before and after reading. This strategy activates or builds students' prior knowledge about a topic, helping them set a purpose for reading so that they can focus their attention on the key information in the text.

There are many ways to create an anticipation guide. The common elements in an anticipation guide are a set of clear directions, a series of statements about major concepts and ideas in the reading selection, and two columns for students to mark agree/disagree, yes/no, or true/false about each statement before and after reading. Figure 5.1 is an example of an anticipation guide on astronomy used in a sixth-grade science class.

Figure 5.1   An Anticipation Guide on Astronomy

Directions: You are going to read about the distance between the Earth and the moon in your text. Carefully read statements #1 and #2 and decide if you agree or disagree with each statement. In the *Before Reading* column, write an A for "agree" and a D for "disagree" before reading the text. When you have completed the reading, you will return to the guide and mark an A for "agree" and a D for "disagree" in the *After Reading* column. For statement #3, write down your educated guess before reading and what the text says after reading. For statement #4, choose the answer that best represents your understanding after reading the text. Be prepared to talk about your answers.

Before Reading		**After Reading**
Agree/Disagree	1. The moon is the Earth's closest neighbor in space.	Agree/Disagree
Agree/Disagree	2. The average distance from the Earth to the moon is 30 times the Earth's diameter.	Agree/Disagree
_____	3. If you are traveling at 100 km/h (60 mph), how long would it take to drive to the moon?	_____

4. How well do you understand the concept of how far the moon is from the Earth?

not at all	a little bit	I think I understand	I know I understand	I'm an expert

Teachers can follow the procedures described below when using an anticipation guide to scaffold student reading:

1. Review the reading selection to identify important ideas and major concepts.

2. Compose 5 to 10 statements about these key ideas and concepts. The number of statements included will depend on the number of concepts to be learned and students' grade level.

3. Write the statements on a poster chart or a sheet of paper, with spaces provided for students to indicate answers (like yes/no, agree/disagree, true/false) or write responses before and after reading. The statements are sequenced in an order that follows the text.

4. Introduce the anticipation guide to students. Have students respond, individually or in small groups, to each statement by indicating what their choices are. As a class, students share and defend their responses to each statement. Their responses to each item can be tallied.

5. Have students read the text. Encourage them to be thinking about how the text relates to the statements in the anticipation guide.

6. Once students are done reading, have them respond to each statement again in light of the text information. Then, students share in small groups or with the whole class what they have learned from reading the text and how their ideas or opinions have changed from before to after reading.

7. Possible extensions: Ask students to choose one statement from the anticipation guide and write a paragraph explaining why they agree or disagree with the statement after reading, using evidence from the text to support their answers.

KWL

KWL is a strategy developed by literacy educator Donna Ogle to get students to think about what they already know about a topic prior to reading and connect it to what they will be learning while reading.[13] The K stands for **Know**; students record what they already know about the topic before reading. The W stands for **Want** to know; students come up with questions they want answered during reading. The L stands for **Learned**; students think about what they have learned from the text after reading. KWL has many permutations. Two of the more popular ones are KWWL (what I **Know**, what I **Want** to know, **Where** I can find the information, and what I have **Learned**) and KWLH (what I **Know**, what I **Want** to know, what I have **Learned**, and **How** can I find the information for questions that are not answered in the text). Figure 5.2 is a KWL chart completed during a science lesson by a third grader as she read about insects in the July, 2006 issue of the *Kids Discover* magazine.[14]

Figure 5.2	KWL Chart on Insects

K (What I Know)	W (What I Want to Know)	L (What I Learned)
Insects are found almost everywhere on the planet.	How many different types of insects are there?	• Scientists believe that there may be as many as three million insect species worldwide.
An insect's body is made up of three segments: head, thorax, and abdomen.	Are spiders insects?	• Spiders are not insects because they only have two main body parts: cephalothorax and an abdomen.
Insects can cause diseases in people, plants, and animals.	Are insects good for us at all?	• Silk and honey are two products we get directly from insects. • Many plants like fruits and vegetables could not survive without insect-related activities.

Procedures for using the KWL strategy and its two variations (KWWL, KWLH) are described below.

1. Prepare a KWL chart. Make a chart with three columns labeled as K (what I know), W (what I want to know or what I wonder), and L (what I learned). Post the chart (if it's large enough) on the classroom wall, or give students a copy of the chart as a handout.

2. Complete the K column. Have students brainstorm what they already know about the topic of the text. During discussion, encourage students to record their own ideas as well as those of their peers. If students are not sure about the information they provide, turn it into a question for inclusion in column W.

3. Complete the W column. This step follows naturally from step K. As students share what they know about the topic, they will have questions that they want to be investigated. Help them use these questions to set the purpose for reading.

4. Complete the L column. Direct students to read the text (or read it aloud to them). Encourage students to stop and record during reading if they find an answer to their questions or an answer that contradicts what they think they already know. Ask students to record the page number and paragraph where they found the answer so that they can go back (if needed) for verification or clarification after reading.

5. Have students check the answers to their questions after reading. This allows them to see what questions are yet to be answered and whether they have additional questions.

6. Variations: KWWL or KWLH. Add Step W (Where I can find the information?) or Step H (How can I find the information?) to the KWL chart. This step enhances students' capacity for research and inquiry. Often students will generate questions that are not answered in the text. After reading, discuss questions that are not answered and brainstorm a list of resources (books, magazines, Internet) where students may find answers. These may even include taking a field trip, conducting an experiment, asking an expert, or bringing in a guest speaker. Encourage students to find the answers and share them with the class.

7. Extension: Ask students to summarize, orally or in writing, the information they have learned from reading about the topic of study.

PKMI

Prior knowledge monitoring and integrating, or PKMI, is a strategy designed specifically for the purpose of correcting misconceptions in prior knowledge.[15] Before reading, students talk about their ideas on a topic. During reading, they check for how their ideas relate to what the text says. After reading, students compare their prior conceptions to what they have learned from the text. A think sheet, such as the one presented in Figure 5.3, is used with the strategy.

What follows is a step-by-step guide for using the PKMI strategy:

1. Introduce the topic of study and present the PKMI think sheet.

2. Have students discuss the central questions in the think sheet and record their ideas in Column I.

3. Have students read the text and complete Column II as they read.

4. After reading, have students place a check in Columns III–VII, whichever is appropriate. Engage students in a discussion about what they have learned from the text and what they have been wondering about. If the text does not address their ideas (Column VII), discuss where they might get further information or why the author did not include that idea in the text. This can be a great segue into a discussion of the biases that may be present in the science text and of how society, technology, and science are interwoven and interconnected to each other.

| Figure 5.3 | A PKMI Think Sheet on Muscles for Seventh Grade |

Central questions	I Everyday ideas I know or believe in	II Scientific ideas from text	III Text ideas same as everyday ideas	IV Text added ideas	V Text conflicts with everyday ideas	VI Text is confusing	VII Text doesn't talk about my ideas
How many muscles do we have?							
What is our strongest muscle?							
How do muscles work in our body?							

MONITORING COMPREHENSION: PROMOTING THINKING DURING READING

One of the more neglected aspects of reading in classroom instruction is the during-reading time. Often, students are asked to talk about a topic before they read and then answer questions after they read. What happens during reading is also important because it determines how well students are able to respond to questions after reading. Reading is not just a matter of eyes taking in printed symbols, but involves active sense making.[16] Teachers need to think about ways to help students slow down and pay attention to whether they are making sense of what they are reading. In this section, we describe three strategies aimed at getting students to think about what they are reading. These strategies are think-pair-share, questioning the author (QTA), and reciprocal teaching.

Think-Pair-Share

Think-pair-share is a strategy that encourages students to talk about what they are thinking during reading.[17] When students read silently, it is difficult to know what is going through their head. Think-pair-share puts two students together to talk about what they are thinking as they read, allowing them to share their responses to the text and make connections with one another so that they develop a richer understanding of text. By making thinking and understanding explicit, students become more aware of—and can better monitor—their own reading processes. During think-pair-share, students work in pairs reading the same selection and at pre-determined points throughout the text they stop to talk about what they are reading.

Presented below is a think-pair-share conversation between two seventh-grade students (Meredith and Judy) in a science class after they have read a section in their science textbook about eclipses.

Meredith: I read this piece on eclipses and I learned that in the middle of the day it can look just like nighttime for a few minutes when a total eclipse happens.

Judy: What is a total eclipse? I wasn't quite sure when I was reading. I know "total" means "whole," but what is an eclipse? I have only heard of that word as the name of a kind of car. I was surprised to see it in science.

Meredith: From what I have just read, I think that eclipse means to cover something. In this case, the sun's light is totally blocked out. Look at this picture in the text. The moon completely covers the sun.

Judy: So what happens on the Earth then? It gets dark, huh? I don't think I've ever noticed that happening. And it says here it can last up to 7.5 minutes. I think I would notice that.

Melissa: Yeah, probably. Maybe it doesn't happen very often. I wonder when it will happen again. I would like to see one. Maybe if we keep reading we will find out. Isn't that cool though?

The following think-pair-share procedure can be used to encourage students to think about what they are reading:

1. Select a text that relates to a current unit of study and identify points in the text where students can stop to talk about

what they are reading. Mark those places in the text so that students can jot down what they want to talk about in the margins.

2. Have students preview the text and predict what it's about. Then draw students' attention to the marked places in the text where they will be stopping to share their thoughts. Alternatively, students can determine for themselves where in the text they would like to stop to talk about their thinking.

3. Students begin to read together, noting the questions or issues each may have on the margins of the text or in their notebooks. At predetermined points in the text, students stop to raise issues, share interpretations, clarify information, make comments, offer predictions, or respond to each other's questions.

4. After students have completed reading and sharing, have the class discuss how sharing their thoughts with a peer during reading helps them understand the text better.

QTA

Questioning-the-Author, or QTA, is a teacher-led strategy that encourages inquiry and critical reading.[18] It engages students in actively processing the text by thinking about the author's intent and ideology. The strategy is especially appropriate for use with texts that deal with socioscientific or environmental issues. For example, publishers of environmental science textbooks often feel compelled to ignore or minimize the coverage of potentially controversial topics or even misrepresent scientific evidence in order not to offend anybody.[19] QTA can help students read these texts critically.

QTA assists students in recognizing that the author has a purpose and a message. Conversation about the text is focused on comparing the author's messages with students' understanding and interpretation of the text. Table 5.2 lists sample prompts that can be used to promote thoughtful discussion and critical reading. They can help students uncover biases in scientific writing and understand that science is a human activity and not a laundry list of indisputable facts for memorization.

Table 5.2	Guiding Discussion Questions for Reading[20]

Goal	Query
Initiating discussion	• What is the author trying to convey? • What is the author's intended message? • What is the author talking about?
Focusing on the author's message	• That's what the author says on paper, but what does it really mean? • Why did the author choose this word, phrase, or sentence? • Why did the author use this particular example?
Linking information	• How does what we are reading relate to what the author has already told us? • What information does the author add here that connects or fits with what was stated earlier? • What information is being left out and why?
Identifying difficulties with the way the author has presented information or ideas	• Does that make sense? • Why does the author have to say it this way? • What would be lost or gained had the author said it in a different way? • Did the author state or explain that clearly? Why or why not? What do we need to figure out?
Encouraging students to refer to the text for clarification or verification	• Did the author give us the answer to that? • Did the author say that explicitly or implicitly?

QTA has three components—planning the implementation, creating queries, and developing discussion. Procedures for implementing the strategy are described below:

1. Planning. Select a grade-level appropriate text that deals with an interesting or potentially controversial topic. Analyze the text by identifying the big ideas and major concepts. Decide where to stop reading in order to initiate queries that may develop into a discussion.

2. Creating queries. Develop sample questions, such as those listed in Table 5.2, that encourage students to think deeply and critically about what they are reading. These questions are

used to assist students in grappling with text ideas and to facilitate group discussion. Make a poster or a bookmark of these
questions so that students can refer to them during reading.
Students can add their own questions to the list.

3. Reading and discussing. Have students read the first segment
   of the text, stopping at a predetermined point to talk about
   what they have read. During the discussion, the teacher models what thoughtful thinking sounds like, encourages students
   to explore the text, interprets or rephrases the ideas students
   are struggling to express, responds to students' comments in
   such a way that draws their attention to certain concepts or
   ideas, provides information to fill in gaps created by the author,
   and summarizes the big ideas before moving on to the next
   segment of the text.

4. Continuing this reading-and-stopping-to-discuss routine until
   the entire text is read. Encourage students to voice their opinions, letting them know that it is okay to have different views
   from the author's.

5. Extension: Invite the author to the class so that students can
   practice the strategy with a live author in front of them. If this
   is not possible, bring in other books or texts that offer a different perspective or interpretation than the one presented in the
   reading selection. Students can also design their own projects
   (like observations, experiments) to verify the information presented in the text.

Reciprocal Teaching

Reciprocal teaching is a cooperative learning strategy that
requires students to work in small groups to think about what they
are reading.[21] Each group reads a common selection, stopping
intermittently to ask questions and clarify understanding. After
the discussion is complete, the group continues to read. Each
student is assigned a role (asking questions, clarifying problems,
summarizing information, making predictions) and is held
responsible for reporting to the group. This strategy has been
shown to improve students' comprehension of challenging reading materials.

Figure 5.4 shows a group of fourth-grade students using the reciprocal teaching strategy in their science class as they read about planets
in the October 2006 issue of *Kids Discover*.[22]

Figure 5.4 Reciprocal Teaching in Action

The leader read aloud the following text excerpt from the *Kids Discover* magazine:

Mercury is the nearest known planet to the Sun. It is three times closer to the Sun than Earth. Mercury is hot.

Questioner: Hmm, I wonder how hot Mercury is. If it's the planet closest to the Sun, then it must be the hottest of all planets.

Clarifier: Well, Mercury is mostly a ball of hot iron; so it must be very hot. But I remember we learned in Mrs. Nelson's class last year that Venus is the hottest planet.

Summarizer: So, Mercury is hot because it is the nearest to the Sun, but it may not be as hot as Venus, which is further away from the Sun.

Forecaster: I think in the next section we will find out exactly how hot Mercury and Venus are and why Venus may be hotter than Mercury.

The leader then continued to read and each student continued to perform his/her role in the reciprocal teaching group. Students conversed about the topic as each role was being executed.

Procedures for using the reciprocal teaching strategy are described below:

1. Teach each of the component strategies (asking questions, clarifying problems, summarizing information, and making predictions) separately before moving students into reciprocal teaching groups. Introduce one strategy at a time by modeling it. For example, read a few paragraphs from a selection and then stop to summarize. Explain to students the purpose and role of the summarizer. Allow students to practice with just summarizing in small groups. Monitor students' understanding of this role. Once students understand the role of summarizer, continue with modeling the other three roles (clarifier, questioner, forecaster) in the same manner.

2. Once students have grasped the purpose and responsibilities of each role, place them into groups of four or five.

3. Assign each student in the group a role and designate one person as the leader. It might be helpful to provide a bookmark that reviews the expectations for each role so that students can refer to it as they work in small groups.

4. Distribute a reading selection and identify places where students should stop and have a reciprocal teaching conversation.

5. Have the leader of the group begin reading the first section of the text out loud. When the leader stops reading, the questioner generates questions about what was read.

6. Have the student who is clarifying detect and discuss the issues that may have come up while questions were being asked.

7. Have the summarizer synthesize what has been read and discussed so far.

8. Have the forecaster make predictions about what will be read next.

9. Once students are comfortable with the procedures, they can choose their own places to read and talk. They can switch roles as they are reading. Teachers need to monitor how groups are working together during reciprocal teaching.

CONSOLIDATING COMPREHENSION: ORGANIZING INFORMATION FROM TEXT

In this section, we present three strategies that are designed to help students organize text information for the purposes of review, recall, and study. These are graphic organizers, SQ3R (Survey, Question, Read, Recite, Review), and two-column note taking.

Graphic Organizer

A graphic organizer is a visual way of organizing information in a text for the purpose of understanding and remembering.[23] It can be used as an after-reading activity to probe (or consolidate) students' understanding of text. It can also be used as a prereading activity to help activate students' prior knowledge, to find out what students already know about the topic, and to identify possible misconceptions. Graphic organizers use a number of visual aids (such as circles, blocks, arrows, lines, boxes) to map out key connections among main ideas and concepts in the text. The boxes or circles are usually connected with words or phrases that verbalize their relationships.

Figure 5.5 is a graphic organizer constructed by a group of eighth-grade students who have completed their reading about photosynthesis.

Figure 5.5   Graphic Organizer on Photosynthesis

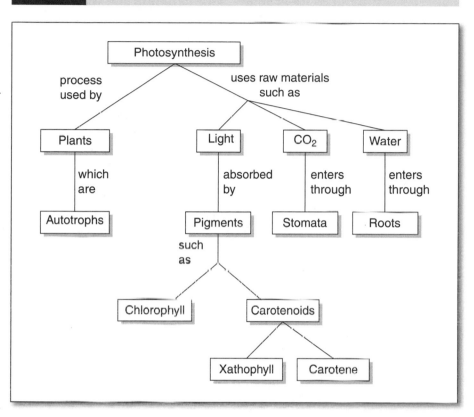

This visual display allows them to summarize, while at the same time visualizing, the key information presented in the text.

The following procedures can be used to help students learn to use graphic organizers to organize the information they glean from text.

1. Select a piece of text that is important and presents information in a complex way.

2. Cue students to the heading, subheadings, pictures, graphs, captions, and topic sentences. Have them predict what the text is about.

3. Have students read the selection. Ask them to identify the major, as well as ancillary, concepts and ideas in the text.

4. Ask students to think about these concepts and ideas and how they relate to each other. Then have students map out key connections among the ideas by using appropriate visual aids (circles, blocks, lines, arrows).

5. Have students use the graphic organizer to review the major concepts and to identify the information in the text that supports them.

SQ3R

SQ3R (Survey, Question, Read, Recite, Review) is one of the most well-known strategies in content-area reading.[24] It helps students organize their thoughts systematically as they read. The strategy consists of the following components:

Survey: Students skim the text, paying attention to titles, pictures, graphs, bold-faced words, subheadings, length of text, and diagrams. This helps students predict what they will be learning about as they read.

Question: Students use the headings and subheadings as natural stopping points to raise and record questions about the text. The headings and the subheadings prompt students to ask questions about the main ideas of the text.

Read: Students read the text to answer the questions they have formulated, jotting down answers as they read to maintain a record of what they are reading. They can add questions as they read.

Recite (or Recall): Students recite answers to their questions during this stage to be sure that they understand the main ideas. They can also talk with a peer or small group about the answers to their questions.

Review (or Reflect): Students review what they have written down and reflect on what they have learned.

Table 5.3 presents a SQ3R worksheet that one sixth-grade student completed while reading a textbook chapter titled "Properties and Changes."[25] The first two sections of the chapter are "Physical and Chemical Properties" and "Physical and Chemical Changes." The subtitles in these sections include physical properties, common physical properties, formation, and states of matter. In the textbook excerpt, there are also pictures of seashells, some tall trees by water, and a glass with water and a straw.

Table 5.3 An SQ3R Worksheet

Questions Based on Headings/Subheadings	Answers from Reading
What are physical properties?	characteristics you can observe without changing the makeup of the material (p. 88)
What are some common physical properties?	color, shape, hardness, smell, taste, texture (p. 88)
How are seashells related to physical properties?	If you look at the seashells, you can notice the physical properties like the shell is hard and some are twisted and some feel rough and some feel smooth. Some are the color of sand and some have designs on them.
Why is formation important?	The physical properties of materials are different because they are formed in different ways. An example is pumice. It is formed from molten rock and it traps a lot of gases so it is light and floats on water, whereas obsidian does not have any trapped gases even though it is formed from the same molten rock, and it is heavier. (p. 89)
What are the states of matter?	a physical property that tells you whether a sample of matter is solid, liquid, or gas (p. 89)

The steps below can be followed when teaching students to use SQ3R:

1. Choose an appropriate reading selection from a unit of study.

2. Introduce students to the strategy by explaining what each letter of the acronym SQ3R means. Post the directions on a poster, if needed.

3. Begin by surveying the text with students. Guide students to make questions out of the subheadings. Record these questions on an overhead or a board.

4. Read the first section of the text with students. Stop and talk about answers to the questions students formulated earlier. Record the answers and ideas. Make sure to also note the page number and paragraph where answers are found so that students can go back to the text later for clarification or verification.

5. Continue reading with students, stopping after each subheading to answer questions and record notes. Students can also do this on their own or with a partner.

6. Immediately after reading each section, have students recite from memory the answers to the questions for that section as well as other important pieces of information they have gleaned from the text.

7. After completing the entire reading selection, have students review their notes and identify main ideas and key concepts in each section. Encourage students to write a brief summary of the reading selection.

Two-Column Note Taking

This is a note-taking strategy that helps students organize the information they have read into a two-column format.[26] Teaching students how to take notes helps them make sense of what they are reading and improves their recall of text information. It also helps students with their writing when they are required to summarize and synthesize information from multiple sources. Students should be encouraged to use their own words when taking notes, instead of copying from the text, so as to avoid plagiarism when writing from these notes. Figure 5.6 is an example of two-column notes taken by a fifth-grade student when he read a text about global warming in his science class.

Figure 5.6	Two-Column Notes on Global Warming

Main Idea	Supporting Details
Global warming causes extreme weather that severely disrupts people's lives.	• We have twice as many severe hurricanes today as what we had 30 years ago. • Arctic sea ice is melting quickly. • Europe was unbearably hot during the summer of 2003. • There was a severe drought in East Africa in 2004. Eleven million people there did not have enough food to eat because of the drought. • A snowstorm in 1993 killed about 300 people in the U.S. and made 10 million people lose electric power.

Specific procedures for teaching the use of the two-column note taking strategy are presented below:

1. Select a text related to the unit of study and review its content.

2. Give students a blank sheet of paper. Instruct them to fold their paper into two columns and write appropriate headings on each one. Column headings can vary (act—opinion, opinion—proof, argument—evidence, for argument—against argument, issue—comment, statement—question, main idea—supporting details) depending on the content of the text and the purpose of the lesson. It might be a good idea to make the left column about one third of the page and the right column larger.

3. If, for example, main ideas and supporting details are chosen as column headings, have students put main ideas on the left column and record supporting details on the right column. Then direct students to read carefully for main ideas as well as supporting details. Encourage students to write in their own words in the right column. A third column can be added to allow students to draw pictures or diagrams that help them better understand and remember the main ideas.

4. After reading, review the main ideas and supporting details that students have included. Encourage them to use their notes to write a summary or study for a test. Additional discussion can include tips for note taking, such as using abbreviations, symbols, and drawings.

PRINCIPLES AND PRACTICE OF READING STRATEGY INSTRUCTION IN SCIENCE

We have described nine reading strategies that promote students' engagement with and comprehension of science texts. When teaching these strategies, it is important for the teacher to not only model strategy use but also provide opportunities for students to practice with authentic texts in the content area. A reading strategy lesson typically includes before, during, and after reading components. In the before-reading component, the teacher introduces and explains the target strategy. In the during-reading component, the teacher models the use of the strategy and guides students to apply the strategy to reading content-area texts. Different types of texts (like textbook, trade book, magazine article) and modes of reading (reading aloud, paired reading, independent reading) can be used. In the after-reading component, the teacher engages students in reviewing the purpose and protocols of the strategy. Follow-up lessons are often needed to allow for further independent practice with the strategy. This explain-model-guide-apply (EMGA) model of strategy instruction ensures that students gain mastery and ownership in using strategies for reading and learning.[27]

Reading strategy instruction is most meaningful and effective when it is embedded in a content area for which it is appropriate. Students benefit when content teachers shoulder some of the responsibilities in teaching reading strategies, instead of leaving them solely to the reading teacher. In fact, as subject specialists, science teachers are in the best position to help students make sense of science texts through infusion of reading strategy instruction. Teaching students how to use reading strategies in the science classroom may seem to take time away from content instruction, but students are in fact learning the content at the same time they are learning the reading strategies if the texts used for strategy instruction are related to the unit of study. Furthermore, once students have developed a repertoire of strategies, they will be able to read with more comprehension and learn content more effectively. In short, time invested in contextualizing reading strategy instruction within the content area will pay off.

To illustrate the above principles of reading strategy instruction, we present in Figure 5.7 and Figure 5.8 two sample lesson plans. What the teacher said during the lesson is italicized. These lessons were developed by two sixth-grade science teachers in collaboration with a team of university-based reading educators.[28] It takes about 20 to 25 minutes to teach each lesson. The first lesson taught students to use thick and thin questions, a questioning strategy for monitoring reading comprehension. The lesson was contextualized in a unit of study called measurement. The second lesson taught students to use two-column note taking for a unit on science biographies. A culminating project for the unit was to write a research paper about a scientist's life or a science career. Students were expected to read science biographies and take notes for use in writing the research paper.

Figure 5.7	Sample Reading Strategy Lesson One

Questioning: Thick and Thin Questions

Science Topic: Measurement of Temperature

Reading Strategy: Questioning: Thick and Thin Questions

Materials: *Temperature: Understanding Science* (pp. 18–21), small and big sticky notes, overhead marker, and transparency

Objective: To encourage students to think about what they are reading and to differentiate between thick and thin questions

Before Reading

Introducing the Strategy

> *Today we are going to learn about thick and thin questions. Will someone tell me what it means to be thick? Thin? Can someone predict what we mean by thick and thin questions?*

Explain what thick and thin questions mean. Write examples of question starters on overhead transparency or chart paper.

> *A thick question asks a big question—one that often leads to deeper discussion or asks you to look beyond the text. You might have to do further research because the answer may not be right there in the text. A thick question addresses big concepts. Often thick questions begin with Why? How come? I wonder? For example: Why is it important for a scientist to be both precise and accurate?*
>
> *A thin question can usually be answered with a simple "yes" or "no," or with a word or phrase. The answer to a thin question may be found right there in the text. These questions are asked to clarify information. If you do not understand a word or are confused by something that the author says, you might ask a thin question. An example would be "What does the word 'precision' mean?"*
>
> *The reason we ask questions about what we read is to help us think about and better understand what we are reading. We want to think today about the different kinds of questions we can ask. As we read the following passage together about measuring temperature, I want you to think about thin and thick questions. I am going to read out loud the first section of this text excerpt on measuring temperature. I want you to follow along. When I stop, I will share with you my thick and thin questions. Be thinking of your own as I read.*

During Reading

Modeling the Strategy

Read out loud Section 1 beginning with the first sentence and ending with "as the temperature changed."

(Continued)

| Figure 5.7 | (Continued) |

As I was reading, my first question was "What is the study of weather?" Is this a thick or a thin question? Why? [Wait for student response.] My next question is "How big was the glass bulb that Galileo put the liquid alcohol in?" My next question is "Where did he get the idea to put this liquid in a tube to measure temperature?"

Discuss question types. Point out to students that thin questions can be answered from the information given in the text. Thick questions push the reader to think beyond the text and to make inferences.

Guided Practice With the Strategy

Guide students to come up with their own thick and thin questions. Give each student one big sticky note and one small sticky note.

I am going to read the next section out loud. As I am reading, I want you to use your big sticky note to write a thick question and your little sticky note to write a thin question about what we read.

Read out loud from "The first mercury . . ." to " . . . than one taken in the shade." Give students time to write their questions. Ask students to share their questions and identify the type of questions they are asking. Write sample questions on transparency or chart paper.

Apply the Strategy Independently

Give students an opportunity to independently read and formulate their own questions.

Now, you are going to read from where I stopped to the end of the selection. As you are reading, jot down at least one thick question on your big sticky note and one thin question on your little sticky note.

Circulate around the classroom to monitor student participation and assist as needed. Once students are done reading and writing, have them share their examples of thick and thin questions with a peer next to them.

After Reading

Ask students to share their questions with the class. As students are sharing, discuss words that signify whether the question is thick or thin. Also discuss what the questions are about, which questions are answered in the text, and where students can find information to answer questions that are not addressed in the text.

Conclusion

Use this time to recap what the lesson is all about.

Today we read a selection about measuring temperature. To help us better understand the selection, we used the strategy of asking thick and thin questions. [Review definitions of each.] Asking thick and thin questions as you read will get you to think about what you are reading and improve your comprehension.

Figure 5.8	Sample Reading Strategy Lesson Two

Two-Column Note Taking

Science Topic: Science Biographies

Reading Strategy: Two-Column Note Taking

Materials: *The Life of Benjamin Banneker,*[29] notebook paper, chart paper, sharpie

Objective: To provide students with a tool for organizing important text information for further review and study

Before Reading

Introducing the Strategy

Begin the lesson by explaining the target reading strategy and stating its purpose.

Today we are going to practice a strategy to help us record and remember important information from the text so that we can use it for our science biography project. Can someone share with me a way that they record information about something they are reading? How do you know what to write down? Is all of the information you read equally important?

Allow a few students to share their responses. Then say,

The strategy we are going to use today is called two-column notes. One thing that is important when you record information from a text is to have a plan or a method for writing down what you think is important for your project. This helps us remember what we have read.

Briefly share your personal methods of note-taking here. Then hand out a blank or lined sheet of notebook paper to students and model how to take two-column notes.

Today, I would like you to try using two-column notes. On your sheet of notebook paper, please create two columns like you see on my overhead transparency. On the left side write FACTS; on the right side write RESPONSES. As we read for information, on the left side under FACTS we record factual information from the text that we think is important for us to know, that is, information that will help us write our biography reports. On the right side under RESPONSES write down your personal response to the piece of factual information you have just recorded. Your response might be a question, or you might write "this reminds me of . . ." or "I wonder why . . ."

During Reading

Modeling the Strategy

Read the first two pages of the book and stop to write down one important fact about Benjamin Banneker's life on the left column of the overhead transparency. Then jot down a question or comment you or your students may have about this piece of information on the right column of the transparency.

(Continued)

Figure 5.8	(Continued)

Guided Practice With the Strategy

Have students practice two-column note taking with your guidance using the piece of notebook paper handed out earlier.

I am going to read a brief excerpt from this book about Benjamin Banneker. As I read, I want you to listen for at least one important fact that you learn about Benjamin Banneker. When I am done, you will record that fact on your note sheet.

Read aloud the text excerpt and then direct students to record a fact once reading is completed. Next, direct students to write a response under the RESPONSES column. While students are participating, record your own response on the overhead transparency.

Now that we have recorded important text information and our responses on our note sheets, let's share what we have written down.

Have students share and discuss their notes in small groups or with the whole class.

Applying the Strategy Independently

Have students read a few more passages on their own and practice recording important facts from the text and their personal responses to each fact. Circulate around the room and provide help as needed.

After Reading

Once reading and recording are completed, have a few students share. Ask students to explain why they feel the information they wrote down is important.

Conclusion

Recap the name and purpose of the focal reading strategy.

Today we have practiced the strategy of two-column note taking. Can someone summarize for me what we did with this strategy? Can someone tell me why a system of taking notes is important for a project like our science biography project?

CONCLUSION

Science texts are challenging to read, and students need support when interacting with these texts. Such support can be provided (a) before reading to help students activate, develop, and integrate relevant background knowledge; (b) during reading to get students to think about what they are reading; and (c) after reading to help students organize and reflect on the information they have gleaned from the text. The reading strategies described in this chapter offer the support students need to effectively engage with, comprehend, and learn from science texts.

6

Learning to Write and Writing to Learn in Science

Throughout this book, we have emphasized the role of language and literacy in science education. We note, for example, that science has evolved a special use of language over the past few centuries to meet its needs and that understanding this language is a vital part of science literacy. We also describe strategies for using trade books to support science inquiry, for helping students cope with the language of science, and for scaffolding student-text interaction. In this chapter, we focus on the role of writing in inquiry-based science, highlighting the need for students to learn to write scientifically and describing an instructional framework as well as practical classroom ploys for promoting the use of writing as a tool for learning science and for enculturation into the scientific community.

WHY WRITE IN SCIENCE?

Writing is an integral part of doing and learning science. Real scientists engage in writing as part of their social practices within the discipline.[1] They write to record the procedures, observations, and results of experiments so that they (and their peers) can check the accuracy, completeness, reliability, and replicability of their findings. They write to reflect on their own work or to synthesize bodies of work in order to develop new ideas. They write to communicate their work to the scientific community for personal and professional benefits. They write to obtain funding or endorsement for their proposed projects. They also write for nonexpert readerships to disseminate scientific information to the public and to engage the public in debates over science issues such as global warming, food safety, and stem cell research. In short, scientists write for a myriad of reasons as part of their trade.

Not only is writing an indispensible vehicle for doing science, it is also a powerful tool for learning science. Writing enables students to connect science with everyday life; to clarify, evaluate, and consolidate understanding; to explore alternative ideas; to solve problems; to develop reasoning, critical thinking, and communication skills; and to acquire new ideas and deeper insights. For example, Canadian researchers Reonard Rivard and Stanley Straw found that writing helps students transform rudimentary ideas into coherent, well-structured knowledge and improves their retention of science learning over time.[2] Other researchers have reported that writing promotes conceptual change and enhances science learning.[3] According to Yore, Hand, and Prain, writing in science provides "an effective context for reflection and consolidation of science understandings initiated during laboratory investigations, lectures, tutorials, reading assignments, and class discussions."[4] In short, writing facilitates science learning in many different ways.

Because of its centrality to doing and learning science, writing is seen as key to disciplinary enculturation. In order to become members of the scientific community, students must learn to write scientifically and to use writing as an epistemological tool for acquiring scientific knowledge, understanding, and habits of mind. We discuss ways to promote such learning in the rest of this chapter.

> *In order to become members of the scientific community, students must learn to write scientifically.*

LEARNING TO WRITE SCIENTIFICALLY

As noted earlier, scientists write for a variety of purposes and audiences. These different purposes and audiences call for different types of writing (lab notes, editorials, research reports) and use of multiple systems of semiotic resources (language, mathematical symbols, visual images). Recent studies found that real scientists engage in the following types of writing as part of their professional practices: journal articles (research reports, research reviews, book reviews, commentaries), lecture notes (handout or web), grant applications, posters, abstracts, letters to the editors of science journals and newspapers, PowerPoint presentations for seminars and talks, operational or procedural manuals, lab and field notebooks, short articles or columns for nonscience publications, web and electronic conferencing with students, and e-mail exchanges with colleagues.[5] Of these types of writing, research reports are "the predominant genre of academic science discourse communities," because they encapsulate "the discipline's norms, values, and ideology."[6] As such, research reports are not only a privileged form of writing that is highly valued in school science, but they are also the kind of writing that presents perhaps the greatest challenge to students.

Basic School-Based Science Genres

In using research reports to communicate their research findings, ideas, and arguments to the scientific community, scientists have to use the terminology and discourse conventions of the genre that the profession has established. An academic research report typically consists of abstract, introduction (including literature review and research questions), methods, results, discussion, references, and acknowledgments. It can be considered a composite, or hybrid, genre that combines five basic school-based science genres (procedural recount, procedure, report, explanation, exposition), with procedural recount typically occurring in the literature review section, procedure in the methods section, report in the results section, and explanation and exposition in the discussion section. Each of these basic science genres uses structures and grammar that are distinct from each other and from those used in everyday language.[7] While the exact form (or textual realization) of a genre can vary from one instance to another and change over time, each genre has evolved some general language patterns that remain relatively stable over time and enable the reader to recognize it as distinct from other genres. To be able to write academic research reports, students must first learn the language patterns characteristic of each of the basic school-based science genres:

- A *procedural recount* records the aim, steps, results, and conclusion of a specific scientific activity already conducted.

- A *procedural text* is a step-by-step instruction of how to conduct an experiment or observation.
- A *report* text can be descriptive or taxonomic. A descriptive report describes the attributes, properties, and behaviors of a single class of things. A taxonomic report organizes information about things by describing taxonomies of classes and subclasses.
- An *explanation* text gives an account of how something works or reasons for some phenomenon. It deals with interactions of factors and processes, rather than a sequence of events, and thus has a process, rather than thing, as its focus. It usually starts with a general statement about the phenomenon in question, followed by a logically organized sequence of explanatory statements.
- An *exposition,* or persuasive (argumentative), text is intended to convince the reader of a point of view, judgment, or theory through the analysis, interpretation, and evaluation of data. In such a text, the writer advances a thesis, introduces background information about the issue in question, presents evidence to support or refute the thesis, and then sums up the position in light of the argument presented.

Table 6.1 summarizes the social purpose, text structure, and grammatical features of each of these five basic school-based science genres. Sample texts for these genres are presented in Table 6.2.

Table 6.1	The Purpose, Structure, and Grammatical Features of Five Basic School-Based Science Genres[8]

Genres	Social Purpose	Text Structure	Grammatical Features
Procedure	To enable a scientific activity (such as experiment or observation) to occur	• Aim • Materials needed • Steps	• Imperative or declarative sentences • Action verbs • Temporal conjunctions
Procedural Recount	To recount in order and with accuracy the aims, steps, results, and conclusion of a scientific activity	• Aim • Record of events • Conclusion	• Declarative sentences • Use of passive voice to suppress actor • Action verbs • Past tense • Temporal conjunctions

Genres	Social Purpose	Text Structure	Grammatical Features
Explanation	To explain how something occurs or is produced	• Phenomenon identification • Explanation sequence	• Technical terms • Nominalizations • Embedded clauses • Process-focused • Mainly action verbs • Passive voice • Logical conjunctions with cause-effect relationships • Use of present and/or past tense
Report	To describe attributes, properties, behaviors, and so on of a single class or entity in a system of things; or to organize information about things into taxonomies of classes and subclasses	• General statement • Description of various aspects of the thing	• Many linking verbs (*be, have*) • Present tense • Some action verbs • Nominalizations • Technical terms • Embedded clauses • Thing-focused • Descriptive language • Language for defining, classifying, and contrasting
Exposition	To persuade the reader to think or act in particular ways	• Thesis statement with background information about the issue at hand • Arguments with supporting evidence • Reinforcement of thesis	• Logical conjunctions • Adjectives and verbs that convey value and judgment • Some technical terms • Different types of verbs (doing, saying, thinking, linking) • Mainly present tense • Frequent use of passive voice to help structure text • Actions are often changed into 'things' (nominalization) to make argument sound more objective and to help with text flow • Words or phrases for comparison and contrast

Table 6.2	Text Samples of Five Basic School-Based Science Genres

Genre	Text Sample
Procedure	**Activity** **Making a simple circuit** You need • a screwdriver • 2 short lengths of insulated copper wire • 2 crocodile terminal clips • a bulb in a bulb holder • a dry-cell battery in a battery holder 1. Check that the ends of the copper wires are uncovered. 2. Connect one crocodile clip to one end of a length of wire. 3. Connect the other end to one side of the bulb holder. 4. Fasten the crocodile clip to one battery terminal. 5. Notice that the bulb does not light up, as there is no circuit (pathway) for the electrons. 6. Now connect another clip to the second wire, and the free wire's end to the other side of the bulb holder. 7. Fasten this crocodile clip to the other battery terminal. 8. What happens? If the electrons can flow around the circuit from the zinc to the carbon the bulb should light. 9. Disconnect one crocodile clip from the battery terminal. 10. What happens to the other bulb? Why? 11. Swap the terminals. Does the battery still work? 12. Draw your complete circuit showing the bulb lit.[9]
Procedural Recount	In February 1997, researchers announced that they had cloned a sheep named Dolly. In the laboratory, they removed the nucleus of an egg cell taken from a female sheep. They replaced that nucleus with the nucleus from a cell of a second breed of sheep. The egg divided and formed an embryo. This embryo was implanted into the uterus of a female sheep of a third breed. Three breeds of sheep were used to show that Dolly received her genes from the transplanted nucleus of the second sheep—not the egg cell donor (the first sheep) or birth mother (the third sheep).[10]
Explanation	Earth's crust is made up of large slabs of rock, called plates. At one time, most of western North America was at or below sea level. Approximately 70 million years ago, the Pacific plate crashed against and slid below the North American plate, creating a 130,000-square-mile area a mile high, called the Colorado Plateau. Aftershocks created the Rocky Mountains. The ancestor of the Colorado River, which had meandered over the plateau before collision, began cascading downhill toward an outlet in the Gulf of California. That was the beginning of the Grand Canyon.[11]

Genre	Text Sample
Report	**Descriptive Report** Hydrogen is the simplest of all the elements. It is also the most common element in the universe. Each hydrogen atom is made up of one proton and one electron. At room temperature, hydrogen is a colorless, odorless gas that is very flammable. Hydrogen is used to make many different chemicals, including fertilizers. It is extracted from natural gas.[12] **Taxonomic Report** No two clouds are exactly the same. Although they vary in shape and size, they can be divided broadly into two similar types: heaped, fluffy clouds; and layered clouds. Heaped clouds are formed when pockets of warm air drift upward, while layered clouds are created by moist air moving horizontally between cooler layers. Clouds are usually grouped according to how high they are above the ground. It is important to identify different types of cloud because they give us information about the weather. White, fluffy cumulus clouds, for example, are associated with warm sunny days. High cirrus clouds mark the approach of a weather front (an advancing mass of warm or cold air). Cirrus clouds may be followed by lower altostratus clouds and low stratus rain clouds, which cover the entire sky in a solid gray sheet.[13]
Exposition	The changes occurring today, however, are primarily the result of human activity. As the world's population has grown, forests have been cut down, prairies plowed under for farms, cities have expanded, and factories and cars have spewed pollution into the air and water. Illegal killing of animals has also increased as some cultures highly value products made from protected animals. Our activities are threatening the existence of many animals; therefore, it is our responsibility to protect those that remain.[11]

According to Robert Veel, these five genres "set up particular kinds of 'knowledge paths' for students, in which one kind of knowing about a topic leads to another kind and then to another."[15] For example, we often start an investigation of a science topic by reviewing relevant research literature. This is followed by designing and conducting experiments. We then verify and discuss our experimental results through reading and examining other research reports. We conclude the study by exploring how the topic in question impacts people and society. In terms of written genres, this sequence of activities is captured in a research report, which proceeds from procedural recount through procedure and report to explanation and exposition.

Genre Teaching Cycle

To learn to write scientifically, students need to become familiar with the purpose, text structure, and grammatical features that characterize each of the five basic school-based science genres identified in Table 6.1. These linguistic features are different from those that construct other parts of the school curriculum[16] and must be explicitly taught in school. Australian sociolinguist James Martin has argued that many students do not just "pick up" the distinctive linguistic features of science genres, and that they need to "work towards a much clearer grasp of the function of language as technology in building up a scientific picture of the world."[17]

To develop students' familiarity with and communicative competence in school-based science genres, a genre teaching cycle has been proposed.[18] The approach provides explicit teaching of school-based genres and associated linguistic features through systematic and complementary use of speaking, listening, reading, and writing. It balances explicit language teaching with opportunities for collaborative and independent work. The genre teaching cycle includes orientation, modeling, joint construction of text, and independent construction of text.

Orientation. In this stage, the teacher (a) identifies major understandings and abilities to be developed in the unit; (b) decides which genre (or genres) is appropriate for developing these abilities and understandings; (c) collects sample texts in the chosen genre from such sources as textbooks, trade books, Internet, magazines, newspapers, and journals; and (d) plans activities (read-alouds, Internet exploration, home reading, lab work) to familiarize students with the topic and immerse them in the target genre.

Modeling. In this stage, the teacher introduces sample texts of the target genre to the class and engages students in an explicit discussion of the genre in terms of its purpose, text structure, and grammatical features per Table 6.1. Helping students recognize these genre features is critical to moving them from "knowledge telling" (texts with random listing of facts) to "knowledge transforming" (texts with rhetorical crafting) in their writing.[19]

Joint Construction. In this stage, using the model texts as a guide, the teacher coconstructs with the whole class texts in the target genre or has students in small groups collaborate to construct texts in the target genre.

Students engage in the process of researching the topic, pooling information together, and jointly contributing to the writing of text.

Independent Construction. In this stage, the teacher has each student independently choose a topic and write a text in the target genre. Students write drafts and make revisions based on comments from their teacher or peers. The comments should address both content (accuracy and completeness of ideas) and form (organization, language use) in the text. Student work can be published periodically in a class newsletter, newspaper, or magazine.

WRITING TO LEARN IN SCIENCE: AN INSTRUCTIONAL FRAMEWORK

Recognizing that academic research reports are not the only type of writing that scientists use in doing science, some science educators[20] have argued for inclusion of other, more informal types of writing in the science curriculum, such as fictional stories (horror, romance, adventures, comic strips), diaries and journals (travelogues, autobiographies), letters (to friends, family members, and newspaper editors), poems (ballads, odes, cinquains), songs (rap, rock), analogies, scripts (radio shows, screen plays), advertisements (brochures, posters), journalistic writing (news and sports reports, editorials), and visuals (sketches, maps, diagrams). They noted that scientists regularly use both formal and informal types of writing to construct and critique scientific knowledge and to communicate their theories and understandings to a wide array of readerships for

> *Scientists regularly use both formal and informal types of writing to construct and critique scientific knowledge and to communicate their theories and understandings to a wide array of readerships.*

varied purposes within and beyond the scientific community. This suggests that learning to use diverse types of writing practices should constitute the process of enculturation into the scientific community.

In response to this perspective on science writing, science educators Vaughan Prain and Brian Hand proposed an interactive-constructivist model of science writing instruction that recognizes "the complex interconnectedness between the demands of different writing tasks and types, subject-topic-task interactions, and student learning outcomes."[21] The model subscribes to the basic principles of constructivism (learners generate knowledge and meaning from their experiences) and is based on the assumption that students will improve science learning if they "write for diverse purposes, varied readerships, in different genres, to meet varied task demands, and with a conscious focus on write-to-learn strategies."[22]

The model identifies five interlocking dimensions of writing as the basis for a matrix for using writing to support science learning. These dimensions are

- topic (key concepts, linking themes, factual understandings);
- genre (procedures, reports, explanation, exposition, stories, scripts, poems, journals, diagrams, letters, concept maps);
- purpose (assess prior knowledge, clarify understanding, classify information, explain an idea, give guidelines or instruction, interpret data, argue for or against a position on an issue, demonstrate understanding, apply knowledge);
- audience (teachers, peers, parents, general public, visitors, consumers, industrial and government agencies); and
- method of text production (individual vs. collaborative work, paper/pencil vs. computer).

This model provides a basis for teachers to plan writing assignments that support science learning. The choices available within each dimension of the matrix allow teachers to calibrate particular combinations that best support student learning of specific topics. The underlying goal of the model is to have teachers diversify the purposes, forms, demands, and audience of writing tasks in the science curriculum.

In order to successfully implement the model, teachers need to nurture functional beliefs about writing and explain the purpose and relevance of each writing assignment; they also need to provide authentic, supportive classroom contexts where writing assignments are appropriately diversified based on the topics of study.[23] In addition to providing opportunities for diversified writing, teachers need to explicitly model for students the process of writing, from planning and drafting through composing and revising to proofreading and publishing.[24] They need to show students how to construct different kinds of text, highlighting how language is used to present information, infuse perspective, and organize texts for different purposes and audiences; they also need to provide concrete criteria for evaluating texts so that students know what makes a piece of writing more or less successful and valued.[25] Finally, teachers need to create positive emotional environments by modeling positive attitudes toward writing and providing thoughtful, constructive feedback to student writing.[26]

IMPLEMENTING THE WRITING-TO-LEARN-SCIENCE INSTRUCTIONAL MODEL

To illustrate how the interactive-constructivist model of writing to learn science can be implemented in the classroom, we describe a fifth-grade lesson on mealworms, spotlighting (in italics) where writing was used to support science inquiry and student learning. The lesson, taught by Mr. Lee, is part of a larger unit through which students learned about the characteristics, life cycles, and interdependence of living things. Prior to the start of the lesson, Mr. Lee had assigned a number of trade books on the topic for his students to take home to read over the weekend. Each student was to have read at least one of these books before the lesson started on Monday. *The students were to write down in their science journals at least two facts about mealworms that they learned from the book and two questions that they wanted answered about mealworms but were not addressed in the book.* The purpose of this informal writing task was to help the students construct understanding of and stimulate their curiosity about mealworms.

When the lesson on mealworms started on Monday, the students, in small groups of four to five, shared their science journals and *completed a concept definition word map on mealworms* (see Chapter 4). The purpose of this writing activity was to activate and assess the students' prior knowledge about mealworms. Mr. Lee went from group to group, listening to the discussion and assisting the students in completing the mealworm word map. After 10 minutes, the teacher gathered the whole class together and had the students suggest a question they would like to inquire about. With about two-thirds of the students expressing an interest in mealworms' response to light, Mr. Lee decided to have his students conduct an investigation to determine how mealworms respond to light. He started the investigation by having the students talk about some of the things that their favorite pets liked and did not like, as well as possible reasons for these likes and dislikes. *He recorded their responses on a chart.* Here, writing was used to highlight the connection between what the students were studying and their everyday life.

Next, Mr. Lee had the students observe mealworms in a glass container and engaged them in a conversation about what mealworms look like. *The students then got back to their original small groups to revise their concept definition word map based on what they had observed about mealworms, such as color, shape, and size.* The purpose of this collaborative writing/revising task was to make sure that the students understood that mealworms are the larva stage of a darkling beetle and that they are cylindrical with an average length of about 1.5 centimeters.

Mr. Lee then had each group write a hypothesis in response to the question "How do mealworms react to light?" and describe possible procedures for testing the hypothesis. This collaborative exercise encouraged the students to make predictions, helping them set a purpose for the subsequent hands-on experiment and giving the teacher insights into their thinking and understanding.

Next, the teacher provided each group with the following materials: eight mealworms, one flashlight, black construction paper, spoon for scooping mealworms, and a transparent container. He instructed the students to observe the following procedures in conducting their investigation:

- Cover one-third of the transparent container with the black construction paper.
- Position the flash light over the exposed area of the container.
- Place eight mealworms in one section of the lighted area and observe the mealworms for five minutes. Record the number of mealworms that move toward the dark area. This is Trial 1.
- Repeat the above procedures two more times.

As the students were conducting the investigation, they also developed charts or graphs to record the number of mealworms moving away from light during each trial. The purpose of this writing task was to record data from the experiment so that the data could be examined and interpreted later. The culminating activity for the lesson involved having students collate the class data, draw a conclusion about how mealworms react to light based on the data collected, and develop an explanation for the conclusion.

As an extension of this lesson for the rest of the week, Mr. Lee had the students explore mealworms' reaction to other environmental factors such as heat, moisture, food, touch, barrier, and sound. *With the teacher's guidance, each group was to pick a factor, research it through reading related trade books and Internet sources, generate hypotheses based on the readings, design and conduct an experiment to verify their hypotheses, and then write a formal research article detailing their hypotheses, experimental procedures, results and interpretations, and conclusions. These articles were to be collected for publication in a special issue of the class journal featuring mealworms. A panel of scientists composed of graduate students in science education would review the articles for their scientific merits and provide feedback.* This writing task consolidated the students' conceptual understanding of the interaction between mealworms and the environment, further developed their inquiry skills, and apprenticed them to the formal writing practices of professional scientists. To prepare students for this writing assignment, Mr. Lee also planned several lessons to explicitly discuss the structural and grammatical features of an academic research paper.

CLASSROOM ACTIVITIES THAT PROMOTE WRITING TO LEARN SCIENCE

Informed by Prain and Hand's interactive-constructive model of writing to learn science,[27] we describe a number of activities for promoting diversified writing practices that support student learning in inquiry-based science classrooms. These activities, which often involve reading and talking, were culled from the professional literature in the fields of science education and literacy education. With minor modifications, they can be used at any grade level. Each unit of study typically calls for the use of several of these activities.

Science Journals

A science journal is a place where students use language and visuals (such as tables, charts, graphs, diagrams, sketches) not only to record, organize, analyze, and interpret data but also to reflect on their experiences in the process of scientific inquiry.[28] Often used synonymously with a science notebook, science journals provide documentation of what students have done, what they are thinking and wondering, what they understand and do not understand, and what they have learned and desire to learn. As such, it is a useful resource for informing instructional planning.

Students will benefit from having clearly articulated guidelines to follow when making journal entries. Michael Klentschy recommended that the following six components be included in science journal entries associated with most, but not necessarily all, lessons:

- Question/Problem/Purpose—Students ask testable questions or state the purpose of the investigation.
- Hypothesis—Students predict what they think will happen as a result of conducting the investigation.
- Planning—Students identify the materials, procedures, variables, and data organizers (table, diagram, graph) related to the investigation.

- Observation/Claims-Evidence—Students record (via words or visuals) what they actually observe and do during the investigation, making sure that all raw data are recorded, instruments or equipments are identified, correct units of measurement are used, correct computations are performed, and all attachments are securely taped to pages.
- "What Have I Learned?"—Students analyze and interpret the results from the investigation, make claims (or draw conclusions) based on the data, and reflect on what they have learned from the process of investigation.
- Next Steps/New Questions—Students ask new questions and describe how they may seek answers to those questions.[29]

To maintain a good science journal, it is also important to label and date each page based on the lesson and assignment. Local scientists can be invited to share their science journals and offer tips for keeping good journal entries. In addition, students should reflect on their journals on a regular basis, using the following questions, suggested by James McDonald and Lynn Dominguez, as a guide: (a) What is something I discovered for the first time? (b) What did I find that surprised me? (c) What happened reminds me of . . . , and (d) What am I wondering about now?[30] Students can also share their reflections with peers in small groups or the entire class.

Learning Logs

While science journal is a formal tool used to record what students do and think during science lessons and lab activities, a learning log is an informal tool for students to document their science learning beyond the science classroom. It encourages students to link school science with their everyday life. In learning logs, students objectively record (via words or visuals) a daily (or weekly) scientific phenomenon, raise questions or wonderings, draw inferences, offer explanations, and make connections to what they are learning in school science. They can also use learning logs to write their responses to a science trade book, a science article, a TV commercial on a science-related topic, or an assignment they are doing in another subject that relates to science in some way.

Once a week, the teacher provides time for students to share with peers (in small groups or with the whole class) what they have written in their learning logs. As students share their logs, the teacher asks probing questions, requests clarifications, gives suggestions, and offers encouragement. Through the weekly sharing, the teacher gains insights into what students are noticing in their surroundings and can plan instruction that fosters inquiry into things that students are interested in and wondering about.

By keeping a log of their daily (or weekly) observations of, responses to, and reflections about their surroundings, students can track their ideas over time and note how their thinking about particular scientific phenomenon or issue evolves. When used in conjunction with science journals, learning logs have the potential to link science with children's everyday life and foster their scientific habits of mind.

Web Logs

Teachers can also capitalize on the power of technology to get students to write to learn science. One way of integrating technology for this purpose is to use "web logs."[31] Web logs are a multigenre, multimedia tool through which the teacher posts a question or a writing prompt and students answer by posting a blog. Students can read and respond to postings by their classmates. As students' postings are filed online, web logs enable students to keep an online portfolio.

> *Web logs are a multigenre, multimedia tool through which the teacher posts a question or a writing prompt and students answer by posting a blog.*

Staycle Duplichan suggested the following steps to help teachers set up a web log in their classrooms.

1. Obtain permissions from school district or principal to use blogging websites in the classroom and from parents for their children's participation in web blogging.

2. Once permissions are obtained, look at examples of web log classroom sites (for example, http://addiference.blogspot.com, http://timlauer.org, www.zimbio.com/Educational+Weblogs, http://anne.teachesme.com, www.leadertalk.org) and decide which example provides the best option to meet your specific needs. The Internet offers free educational web-log sites for students (www.blogger.com/start, www.21classes.com, www.bravenet.com/webtools/journal/index.php, http://edublogs.org, http://classblogmeister.com, http://clearblogs.com).

3. Create an account for each student. Most web logs only require typing in username, password, and student's name. Review Internet safety issues with students, and remind them of proper posting etiquette and logging rules.

4. Start with your home page by writing a message for your students.

5. Consider how student postings are to be assessed. The rubrics for assessment will depend on the nature of the class assignment.[32]

Web logs can be used in many different ways to encourage students to write to learn science. For example, students can write about current news events involving science, pose questions about a science topic they are studying, discuss their favorite science trade books, share their research findings from an investigation, compose imaginative writing about a science concept, debate a controversial science issue, or post lab results or data for comparison.

Multimodal Writing Projects

"Multimodal Writing Project"[33] zeroes in on students' fascination with multimedia products by encouraging them to produce science writing that purposefully embeds visual elements such as pictures, graphs, images, and diagrams to enhance communication. Integrating visuals within a written text is a common strategy used by scientists.[34] Teachers can use the following steps suggested by Mark McDermott to plan a multimodal writing project:

1. Show students writing samples from such sources as textbooks, trade books, magazines, newspapers, journals, travel brochures, and museum guides, and engage them in a discussion of how the visuals in these texts complement language in scientific meaning making.

2. Have students identify the strategies the author uses to link the information presented in language to the information conveyed through visual elements. Some of the strategies scientists use in their writing include placing the visual near the text that deals with the related concept, referring to the visual in the text (example: *Please refer to Table 1, as shown in Figure 14–7*), and inserting a caption with the visual to summarize what it describes.

3. Students develop a checklist for use to evaluate a multimodal product by determining whether visuals are effectively embedded with language to create a well-integrated written product.

4. Students create small-scale models of well-integrated multimodal products, such as posters, to share with class. The teacher and students provide feedback.

5. Once students become comfortable with multimedia presentation of information, they can then create their own drafts of
multimodal text and use the checklist to assess their own level
of language-visual integration.[35]

Class Publications

Creating a class publication—such as a newspaper, magazine,
journal, or newsletter—allows students to demonstrate their learning
and the teacher to assess student learning in a unit of study. In writing for the class publication, students will have to synthesize and
apply what they have learned by producing a piece of creative literature (like research articles, comic strips, advertisements, poems, editorials, travel guides, commentaries, book reviews, news reports).
They also need to consider the audience and purpose of their writing.
The following steps, adapted from Amy Robertson and Kathryn
Mahlin,[36] can be used to help develop a class publication:

1. Introduce the idea of creating a class publication (like a
newsletter for younger students or a newspaper or magazine/
journal for older students) at the end of a unit of study. Have
students discuss the different parts that make up the publication. Show students publication samples to familiarize them
with the format of the publication. The editor of a local publication (newspaper, newsletter, magazine, journal) can be
invited to share tips about writing for the publication.

2. Have students decide what sections they would like to include
in the publication. List the section topics on board.

3. Divide students into groups of three to five, and have each
group choose a section to write. If more than one group is com-
peting for the same section, a drawing can be held. Alternatively,
students can indicate first or second preference for their choices.

4. Have the class brainstorm the types of information to be
included in each section of the publication. As the class gives
suggestions for the topics in each section, the group responsible for writing that section will take notes.

5. With teacher input, the class as a whole creates an assessment
rubric to help guide students through the assignment. Some
of the assessment criteria can include content accuracy and
depth, creativity, discourse styles and conventions, and language mechanics.

6. Students in each group write their section of choice. In order to write the section, they will first need to identify relevant resources (trade books, magazines, journals, Internet). Once resources are collected, they divide up the reading assignments and take notes during reading. If needed, a lesson on note taking can be taught (see Chapter 5). Students can also draw on the information they have gathered in their science journals or learning logs to help with their writing.

7. Students review each other's notes and determine what information is relevant to the task at hand. (The teacher can also review the notes to give feedback.) Students then start writing their chosen section collaboratively. They are encouraged to incorporate other media (pictures, diagrams) to enhance their writing. Once the first draft is finished, it can be revised, edited, and refined. Each group can also schedule a conference with the teacher to get feedback and guidance for their writing.

8. Each group presents their section to the entire class. The class as a whole gives feedback, which allows the group to make final changes to the writing before it goes into press.

Biography Book Projects

In a biography unit, students can create a book on a scientist of their choice. The complexity of the book depends on students' grade level. For younger students, simple pop-up books would be appropriate.[37] For older students, more comprehensive biographies are expected. Students can work on a book individually or collaboratively. The purpose of the book project is to introduce students to a scientist and to highlight a particular scientific habit of mind illustrated in that person's life. The project can help students learn about science at the same time they are learning about the scientists who interest them.

Rebecca Monhardt suggests that the following process be used to help students create biography books.[38] Before the writing begins, the teacher engages students in a discussion of key scientific habits of mind, such as curiosity, open-mindedness, desire to learn and discover, critical mindedness, demand for accuracy and precision, accepting ambiguity, and logical reasoning. Students are then provided many biographies so that they can read them in school or at home. They then select a scientist whose life story they will use to create their book and complete a short information form where they list the name of the scientist selected, why this scientist is of interest, three sources they have consulted to find information about this scientist, and the particular scientific habit of mind that will be exemplified in the biography.

After students have read several books and gathered information about their chosen scientists, they can begin writing the text (and maybe also creating illustrations) for their book. Students can read each other's drafts and offer feedback in small groups. They can also schedule individual or group conferences with the teacher to review their drafts. Once students are satisfied with their final drafts, they begin to create a book out of their writing. Students may need to be taught how to make a book with paper. Many websites (such as www.mothteeth.com/bookmaking/, http://robertsabuda.com/pop makesimple.asp, www.makersgallery.com/joanirvine/howto.html) provide detailed instruction for making books. Binding a book is in itself a problem-solving process not unlike those undertaken by scientists. Once the books are bound, students can share them with the class or read them to younger children. A rubric for evaluating these student-made biography books can be created collaboratively by students and their teacher.

Science Fair Projects

Science fairs have a long history in American science education. They are exhibitions (or competitions) where students present their science projects in the form of a research report. To prepare for science fairs, the teacher guides students through the steps of conducting an empirical scientific inquiry throughout the school year by having them identify a problem to investigate, conduct background research, and engage in hypotheses testing. During each step of the inquiry process, the teacher guides students in writing a part of what culminates as a research report—abstract, introduction, research question, hypothesis, materials, procedures, results, discussion, and conclusion. Toward the end of the school year, a showcase is held, where students present their work in the form of a research report, display board, and models they have created.

Science fairs provide an opportunity for students to learn the terminology and discourse conventions of traditional research reports. The teacher can adopt the genre teaching cycle discussed earlier in the chapter to guide students in drafting, revising, and refining each component of a research report.

A follow-up to the science fair project is to have students choose a peer's research report and write a formal critique of the report addressing such issues as the replicability of experimental proce-dures, the rigor of analysis, and soundness of the conclusion.[39] This process can teach students to be critical consumers of the science research literature. Students can also be encouraged to compose a col-umn based on their research report for a school newspaper or maga-zine. This exercise should lead students to consider different forms of writing and what it means to write for different readerships.

Mystery Box Writing

"Mystery Box Writing"[40] is an activity that promotes inquiry through questioning, discussing, and writing. It can be used to intro-duce a new unit of study or to revisit topics previously covered. When used at the beginning of a unit, the activity helps students acti-vate prior knowledge and gives the teacher an idea about what students know and do not know about the topic. When used at the end of a unit, it enables the teacher to assess student learning.

The activity begins with the teacher bringing a mystery object or an organism (like beetles, mealworms, screws, plants, rocks, models of body parts) into the classroom, hidden in a box. The teacher then encourages students to guess at the content of the mystery box by asking three types of questions:

1. Does it _____? Can it _____? (use verbs),

2. Does it have _____? Is it a _____? (use nouns), and

3. Is it _____? (use adjectives).

Their guesses are recorded on chart paper. As students ask ques-tions, they can periodically stop to write or draw predictions based on what they know so far. If they are not able to identify the content of the mystery box, they will have to analyze their questions and answers to see what has led them astray. It is this continuous process of asking and refining questions that leads scientists to discover mysteries.

Once the mystery object or organism is identified, students in small groups write about it in any form they deem appropriate. They can choose to create a fictional story or a poem, write a riddle, draw a picture, list several facts, or make a concept definition word map.

E-Pal Projects

Students can further their science learning by writing to real sci-entists such as university professors and graduate students of science and engineering or researchers at research centers.[41] Having students e-mail a scientist about their questions can generate excitement for students. Students can also interview scientists about how they became scientists. If possible, the teacher can arrange for students to visit the lab of their e-pal scientists. By regularly communicating with scientists, students become less intimidated by science and scientists and are more willing to consider science for a career.

Writing Refutational Texts

A refutational text is a kind of persuasive (exposition) writing used to refute a science misconception. It has been suggested that reading and writing refutational texts can help students overcome science misconceptions and increase understanding and retention of the content.[42] Teachers can usually identify students' misconceptions by listening to their discussion and reviewing their work (concept maps, science journals, learning logs).

To get students started on the writing task, teachers can present a prompt that describes a common misconception (such as Batteries have electricity in them. An object at rest has no energy. One degree of temperature is smaller on the Celsius and Kelvin scales than on the Fahrenheit) and have students respond to the prompt by writing a refutational text. An effective refutational text introduces a misconception, refutes it, offers alternative concept/idea/theory, and then supports the new concept/idea/theory/claim with evidence. In writing a refutational text, students may have to check different sources (textbooks, trade books, journal/newspaper articles, websites), synthesize and organize the information they have read, and even collect their own evidence through hands-on observation or experiments.

Analyzing Analogies

An analogy is a linguistic expression that relates two things (concepts, ideas) that are in some respects similar. In an analogy, one thing that is less familiar (called "target") is compared to another thing that is more familiar (called "analog"). For example, the analogy that "a cell is like a city" compares the new concept "cell" to the familiar concept "city," making the new concept easier to understand, visualize, and remember. Thus, analogies allow the teacher to put new or abstract concepts and principles in familiar terms that students can more easily understand. They are especially useful in helping students understand difficult science concepts and may stimulate students' interest in learning these concepts.[43]

Analogies can provide the focus for an inquiry activity, enabling the teacher to assess students' understanding of newly introduced concepts.[44] For example, the teacher can give students an analogy (An atom is like a bookcase; Endothermic and exothermic reactions are like a sponge and water; A cyst is like a balloon with water or pudding in it; Fiber in your diet is like a sponge; The external ear canal is like conveyor belt) and have them analyze the analogy by writing an explanation of the similarities and differences between the analog and the target (new concept). Students can also write an argument about why an analogy (Glucose is like cars on the freeway. Fever is not a part of the disease any more than red lights and sirens are a bank robbery. Eating food with calcium is like adding to your savings account. Is the lock-and-key model a good analogy for enzyme action? Is DNA more like a recipe or a computer?) makes or does not make sense. Such analysis often involves research (such as reading relevant books and web pages in search of evidence to support claims) and logical reasoning. Students can respond to an analogy in their science journal or learning log and share their responses in class. The sharing will promote debate and critical thinking, deepening students' understanding of new or abstract concepts.

Science Writing Heuristic

Science Writing Heuristic (SWH) is a writing-to-learn strategy that helps students construct understanding during lab activities.[45] It provides semistructured templates for teacher and student that engage both in negotiating meaning during laboratory investigations. The teacher template includes a set of ideas to assist teachers in designing activities before, during, and after the laboratory work to enhance students' understanding of the target concepts. For example, it is recommended that the teacher examines students' understanding before and after instruction through individual or group concept mapping and prepares students for the lab work through the informal tasks of observing, note taking, brainstorming, and questioning. As students engage in laboratory work, the teacher encourages students to write journal entries, compare data and interpretations, verify conclusions with other sources of materials (like textbooks), and reflect on the process of investigation.

The student template includes a number of questions that guide students to produce written explanations of the processes involved in the lab work. The questions are

1. Beginning ideas: What are my questions?

2. Tests: What did I do?

3. Observations: What can I claim?

4. Evidence: How do I know? Why am I making these claims?

5. Reading: How do my ideas compare with other ideas?

6. Reflection: How have my ideas changed?[46]

These questions are intended to help students interpret data and make meaningful connections among procedures, data, evidence, and claims.

In essence, SWH is an instructional strategy that enables the teacher to help students make sense of their data; construct and support knowledge claims; and provide linkage between data, claims, and evidence. It emphasizes three key ingredients of scientific inquiries— claims, evidence, and reflection. Research has demonstrated the effectiveness of the strategy in enhancing students' conceptual understanding and scientific reasoning.[47]

Concept Mapping

Concept mapping promotes writing and discussion that can lead to deeper conceptual understanding.[48] Hand, Prain, Lawrence, and Yore suggest the following process for using concept maps to enhance science learning.[49] The teacher starts the activity by reading a trade book related to the unit of study and then has students in groups develop a detailed map about a key concept in the unit. Through class discussion and negotiation, group maps are integrated into a single complex class map. In order to construct the class map, students have to explain their reasoning and justify their sense of knowing. Students then analyze the integrated class map to clarify understanding and build scientific terminology associated with the essential components of the concept. Next, students, individually or in small groups, pick an aspect of the integrated class map for further exploration (such as through reading or hands-on investigation). As an expert on their chosen topic, students then develop a formal report for presentation to the class using language that their peers can understand.

Cubing

Cubing is a writing strategy that encourages students to explore a topic (concept, object, organism) from multiple angles.[50] Students examine a topic (represented by a cube, or square prism) from six angles, with each angle representing one side of the cube:

1. *Describe* the topic, including its color, shape, size, touch, and smell (whichever is applicable).

2. *Compare* the topic to something else by considering how they are similar or different.

3. *Associate* the topic with something else by discussing how the topic connects to other subjects or issues.

4. *Analyze* the topic by describing how it is made or what it is composed of.

5. *Apply* the topic by explaining how it can be used and what can be done with it.

6. *Argue* for or against the topic by taking a stance and giving reasons for it.

Each student in a group (or each group in the class) can take one of the sides and discuss it (or write about it) for five to ten minutes. Students then get together to share what they have written or discussed in relation to their sides. The information generated from these writing or discussion sessions can become the basis for more extended writing assignments involving the topic.

Quickwrites

Quickwrites is a strategy for engaging students in impromptu writing about a topic or concept prior to and after a lesson or unit.[51] It is an effective way for students to activate prior knowledge before the lesson and demonstrate their learning after the lesson. It also allows the teacher to gauge student knowledge about a topic before and after the lesson.

Quickwrites is structured by the teacher and done in a short amount of time (five to ten minutes), during which students individually write down as much as they know about the topic. Writing can be done in a journal, note card, handout, or regular paper. Students share what they have written in small groups or with the entire class. They also compare what they wrote before and after the lesson and discuss changes in their understanding of the topic.

Others

In addition to the activities described above, there are many other ways of engaging students in writing to learn in the science classroom. For example, some science educators have suggested that students can use various forms of imaginative writing to help them learn science.[52] Some of their ideas for writing include the life story of a chromosome or a blood cell, a poem about a monotreme, an anthropomorphic narrative about a water molecule, a survival guide, guides to the use of certain materials or equipment, a travel brochure advertising a trip to another planet, a realistic recount of the forces that a parachutist experiences throughout a jump, and stories about a scientist's life or a particular scientific invention. Thomas Turner and Amy Broemmel also suggest a list of possible writing activities in the science classroom, which include hypothetical letters between scientists to exchange ideas, case reports detailing a chain of evidence that leads to the arrest and trial of a suspect in an imaginative crime, accident reports involving collection of evidence, directions from one location to another, analysis of the information contained or not contained in consumer product labels, grant proposals for class projects, and news clip observations.[53] These activities diversify students' writing experiences and are aimed at improving their science learning.

CONCLUSION

Writing is both a form of social practice in science and a vehicle for learning science. It provides students "an occasion to think through arguments and to master forms of reasoning and persuasion that are valued in various disciplines" including science.[54] Like reading, writing is integral to doing and learning science and central to disciplinary enculturation. In fact, science and reading and writing are more than supportive and synergistic; they are "isomorphic" and deeply intertwined.[55] Thus, if the goal of science education is the development of science literacy for all students,

> Like reading, writing is integral to doing and learning science and central to disciplinary enculturation.

science teachers must be proactive in using language and literacy practices to support science teaching and learning. As Wellington and Osborne implored,

> We [science teachers] are, primarily, raconteurs of science, knowledge intermediaries between the scientific canon and its new acolytes. Such an emphasis means that we must give prominence to the means and modes of representing scientific ideas, and explicitly to the teaching of *how to read, how to write and how to talk* science.[56] (emphasis in original)

Endnotes

Chapter 1

1. National Research Council (1996); Rutherford & Ahlgren (1990)
2. Grigg, Lauko, & Brockway (2006)
3. Gonzales, Williams, Jocelyn, Roey, Kastberg, & Brenwald (2008)
4. Osborne, Simon, & Collins (2003)
5. Lemke (2001, p. v)
6. American Association for the Advancement of Science (1993); National Research Council (1996, 2000)
7. Hand, Alvermann, Gee, Guzzetti, Norris, Phillips, et al. (2003); Saul (2004); Wellington & Osborne (2001); Yore, Hand, Goldman, Hildebrand, Osborne, Treagust, et al. (2004)
8. National Research Council (1996)
9. American Association for the Advancement of Science (1993)
10. National Research Council (2000, p. 13)
11. Chiappetta & Adams (2004)
12. Crawford (2007, p. 614)
13. National Research Council (2000, p. 13)
14. National Research Council (1996, p. 22)
15. Colburn (2008); Hmelo-Silver, Duncan, & Chinn (2007); Shymansky, Kyle, & Alport (1983); Wise & Okey (1983)
16. Wilson, Taylor, Kowalski, & Carlson (2010)
17. Chang & Mao (1999)
18. Dalton, Morocco, Tivnan, & Mead (1997)
19. Hmelo-Silver, Duncan, & Chinn (2007, p. 104)
20. Bell, Smetana, & Binns (2005); Crawford (2007)
21. Abd-el-khalick, F., Boujaoude, S., Duschl, R., Lederman, N., Mamlok-Naaman, R., Hofstein, A., et al. (2004); Anderson (2002); Crawford (2007)
22. Hudson, McMahon, & Overstreet (2002); Weiss, Pasley, Smith, Banilower, & Heck (2003)
23. Bybee, Powell, & Trowbridge (2007); Minstrell & van Zee (2000); National Research Council (2000); National Science Foundation (1999)
24. Bunce (2002)
25. Crawford (2000, p. 933)
26. Bell, Smetana, & Binns (2005, p. 33); Fay & Bretz (2008, p. 41)
27. Flanagan (2000)

28. Chasek (2000)
29. Kittinger (1997)
30. Symes (2004)
31. Horenstein (1993)
32. Zim & Shaffer (1985)
33. Johnson (2004)
34. Baldwin (2004)
35. Oxlade (2002)
36. Hand, Alvermann, Gee, Guzzetti, Norris, Phillips, et al. (2003); Saul (2004); Yore, Hand, Goldman, Hildebrand, Osborne, Treagust, et al. (2004)
37. Norris & Phillips (2003)
38. Halliday & Martin (1993); Martin & Veel (1998)
39. Norris & Phillips (2003, p. 226)
40. Wellington & Osborne (2001, p. 117)
41. Glynn & Muth (1994); Rivard (1994); Yore, Bisanz, & Hand (2003)
42. Palinscar & Magnusson (2001)
43. Wellington & Osborne (2001)
44. Yore, Hand, & Florence (2004)
45. Fang (2005, 2006, in press)
46. Craig & Yore (1995)
47. Perie, Grigg, & Donahue (2005)
48. Cervetti, Pearson, Bravo, & Barber (2006); Fang & Wei (2010); Fellows (1994); Gaskins, Guthrie, Satlow, Ostertag, Six, Byrne, et al. (1994); Guthrie, Van Meter, Hancock, Alao, Anderson, & McCann (1998); Key, Hand, Prain, & Collins (1999); Mason & Boscolo (2000); Morrow, Pressley, Smith, & Smith (1997); Rivard & Straw (2000); Romance & Vitale (1992)
49. Hand, Alvermann, Gee, Guzzetti, Norris, Phillips, et al. (2003, p. 614)

Chapter 2

1. Wellington & Osborne (2001, p. 59)
2. M. Brown (2004, pp. 174–177)
3. Sands (2006d, p. 4)
4. Kintsch (2004)
5. Gee (2001)
6. Veel (1997)
7. Glencoe/McGraw-Hill (2000b, p. 584).
8. Halliday (1998)
9. Glencoe/McGraw-Hill (2000b, p. 674)
10. Halliday & Matthiessen (2004)
11. The classification of clause types used in this table is based on Schleppegrell & Colombi (1997), who based their work on Halliday's (1994) functional grammar. For the sake of simplicity, traditional grammar terms "subordinate clauses" and "coordinate clauses" are used here in lieu of the less familiar functional grammar terms "hypotactic clauses" and "paratactic clauses," respectively. For a more fine-tuned distinction of these clause terms, please refer to Schleppegrell and Colombi (1997).
12. Halliday & Martin (1993)
13. Christie & Derewianka (2008)
14. Glencoe/McGraw-Hill (2000b, p. 401)

15. Fang, Schleppegrell, & Cox (2006)

16. Fang (2005, 2006, in press); Fang, Schleppegrell, & Cox (2006); Fang & Schleppegrell (2008)

17. Urban (2007, p. 160)

18. Glencoe/McGraw-Hill (2000a, 2000b)

19. Piddock (2008); Pobst (2008)

20. Glencoe/McGraw-Hill (2000a, p. 36)

21. Chall, Jacobs, & Baldwin (1990)

22. Norris & Phillips (2003)

23. Veel (1997)

24. Lemke (1998, 2000, 2002); Kress (2003); Kress, Jewitt, Ogborn, & Tsatsarelis (2001); Unsworth (1997a, 2001); O'Halloran (2004, 2005); Prain & Waldrip (2010)

Chapter 3

1. Anderson (2004); Hirsch (2006)

2. Kintsch (2004)

3. Yager (2004, p. 95)

4. Wellington & Osborne (2001, p. 112)

5. Cervetti & Barber (2009, p. 39)

6. Perera (2005)

7. Straits & Nichols (2006)

8. Creech & Hale (2006)

9. King (1990)

10. Hadaway, Vardell, & Young (2001)

11. King (1990)

12. Zales & Unger (2008)

13. Daniels (1994)

14. Straits (2007, pp. 33–34)

15. Fang, Lamme, Pringle, Patrick, Sanders, Zmach, et al. (2008)

Chapter 4

1. Halliday & Martin (1993)

2. Halliday & Martin (1993)

3. Wellington & Osborne (2001, p. 139)

4. Duke (2000)

5. Fang (2002); Moss & Newton (2002); Moss (2008)

6. Duke (2004); Young, Moss, & Cornwell (2007)

7. Derewianka (1990, p. 66)

8. Fang (2008); Kamil & Bernhardt (2004)

9. Craig & Yore (1995)

10. Yore & Treagust (2006, p. 296)

11. Ivey & Broaddus (2001)

12. Wade & Moje (2000); Wellington & Osborne (2001)

13. See, for example, Fang, Lamme, Pringle, Patrick, Sanders, Zmach, et al. (2008) for a detailed description of procedures for managing a home science reading program within an inquiry-based science curriculum.

14. P. Robinson (2005, p. 443)
15. P. Robinson (2005, p. 443)
16. Fang (2006)
17. Fang (2006)
18. Fang (2006)
19. Fang (2006)
20. Schwartz & Raphael (1985)
21. Haggard (1986)
22. Fisher, Brozo, Frey, & Ivey (2011); Vacca, Vacca, & Mraz (2011)
23. Lambert (1997, p. 36)
24. Oldfield (2002, p. 94)
25. Miller (2004, p. 423)
26. Unsworth (1997b)
27. Fang (2006)
28. Sands (2006d, p. 13)
29. Glencoe/McGraw-Hill (2000a, p. 579)
30. Halliday (1998); Halliday & Martin (1993)
31. Glencoe/McGraw-Hill (2000a, p. 495)
32. Glencoe/McGraw-Hill (2000b, p. 510)
33. Walker (2003, p. 35)
34. Parker (1992, p. 8)
35. Pobst (2008, p. 31)
36. Gallant (1998, p. 10)
37. Unsworth (1997b)
38. Fang (2006)
39. Scott Foresman (2000, p. C67)
40. Oldfield (2002, pp. 16–17)
41. Murphy (2003, p. 137)
42. Wellington & Osborne (2001); Yore, Hand, Goldman, Hildebrand, Osborne, Treagust, et al. (2004)
43. Schleppegrell (2004)
44. Fang (2006)
45. Wellington & Osborne (2001)
46. Walker (2003, p. 38)
47. Glencoe/McGraw-Hill (2000b, p. 400)
48. Barnitz (1998)
49. Lemke (1989)
50. Unsworth (1997b)
51. Miller (2004, p. 239)
52. Halliday (1998)
53. Reif & Larkin (1991, p. 756)
54. Yore & Treagust (2006, p. 292)
55. Halliday & Matthiessen (2004); Halliday & Martin (1993)
56. Fang & Schleppegrell (2010); Schleppegrell, Greer, & Taylor (2008)
57. Veel & Coffin (1996, p. 225)
58. See, for example, Alvermann, Phelps, & Gillis (2010) and Vacca, Vacca, & Mraz (2011).
59. See, for example, Beers (2002), Keene & Zimmermann (2007) and Fisher, Brozo, Frey, & Ivey (2011).

Chapter 5

1. Alvermann & Moore (1991)
2. Fang (2008); Hirsch (2006)
3. Pressley (2004, p. 420)
4. Wellington & Osborne (2001, p. 117)
5. Alvermann & Moore (1991); Biancarosa & Snow (2004); National Reading Panel (2000); RAND Reading Study Group (2002)
6. R. Brown, Pressley, van Meter, & Schuder (2004, p. 1000)
7. Almasi (2002)
8. Fang & Wei (2010); Gaskins, Guthrie, Satlow, Ostertag, Six, Byrne, et al. (1994); Griffin, Simmons, & Kameenui (1991); Romance & Vitale (1992)
9. Harvey & Goudvis (2007)
10. Frisch (2003)
11. Hirsch (2006)
12. Bean, Readence, & Baldwin (2008)
13. Ogle (1986)
14. Sands (2006b)
15. Dole & Smith (1989)
16. Smith (1996)
17. Lyman (1981)
18. Beck, McKeown, Hamilton & Kucan (1997)
19. Jones (2006)
20. This table was adapted from Beck, McKeown, Sandora, Kucan, & Worthy (1996, p. 390).
21. Palinscar & Brown (1984)
22. Sands (2006c)
23. Pehrsson & Robinson (1985)
24. F. Robinson (1946)
25. Glencoe/McGraw-Hill (2000a)
26. Palmatier (1973)
27. Fang, Lamme, Pringle, Patrick, Sanders, Zmach, et al. (2008)
28. Fang, Lamme, Pringle, Patrick, Sanders, Zmach, et al. (2008)
29. Bedini (1984)

Chapter 6

1. Turner & Broemmel (2006); Wellington & Osborne (2001); Yore, Hand, & Prain (2002); Yore, Hand, & Florence (2004)
2. Rivard & Straw (2000)
3. Fellows (1994); Mason & Boscolo (2000); Warwick, Stephenson, & Webster (2003).
4. Yore, Hand, & Prain (2002, p. 673)
5. Yore, Hand, & Florence (2004); Yore, Hand, & Prain (2002)
6. Yore, Hand, & Florence (2004, p. 339)
7. Martin (1989); Schleppegell (2004)
8. This table was adapted from Veel (1997, p. 172).
9. Catherall (1990, p. 19)
10. Glencoe/McGraw-Hill, (2000b, p. 543)

11. Sands (2006a, p. 4)
12. Oxlade (2002, p. 20)
13. Ellyard (1996, p. 20)
14. Pobst (2008, p. 19)
15. Veel (1997, pp. 173–174)
16. Fang & Schleppegrell (2008); Schleppegrell (2004)
17. Halliday & Martin (1993, p. 202)
18. Derewianka (1990); Unsworth (2001)
19. Bereiter & Scardamalia (1987); Myhill (2009)
20. Hand, Prain, Lawrence, & Yore (1999); Hildebrand (1998); Prain (2006); Prain & Hand (1996)
21. Prain & Hand (1996, p. 618). See also Hand, Prain, Lawrence, & Yore (1999)
22. Prain & Hand (1996, p. 623)
23. Bruning & Horn (2000)
24. Calkins (2004)
25. Fang & Wang (in press); Schleppegrell (2004)
26. Bruning & Horn (2000)
27. Prain & Hand (1996)
28. Mesa, Klosterman, & Jones (2008)
29. Klentschy (2005)
30. McDonald & Domingez (2009, p. 48)
31. Duplichan (2009)
32. Duplichan (2009)
33. McDermott (2010)
34. Lemke (2002); Yore, Hand, & Florence (2004); Yore, Hand, & Prain (2000); Prain & Waldrip (2010)
35. McDermott (2010)
36. A. Robertson & Mahlin (2005)
37. Monhardt (2005)
38. Monhardt (2005)
39. B. Robertson (2005)
40. Straits (2005)
41. Akerson & Young (2005)
42. Dlugokienski & Sampson (2008); Guzzetti, Snyder, Glass, & Gamas (1993)
43. Duit (1991)
44. Glynn, Duit, & Thiele (1995); Orgill & Thomas (2007)
45. Hand & Key (1999)
46. Hohenshell & Hand (2006, p. 271)
47. Hohenshell & Hand (2006); Key, Hand, Prain, & Collins (1999)
48. Novak (1998)
49. Hand, Prain, Lawrence, & Yore (1999)
50. Tompkins (2009)
51. Bean, Readence, & Baldwin (2008)
52. See, for example, Prain & Hand (1996); Hildebrand (1998).
53. Turner & Broemmel (2006)
54. Resnick (1987, p. 38)
55. Cervetti, Pearson, Bravo, & Barber (2006)
56. Wellington & Osborne (2001, p. 138)

References

Abd-el-khalick, F., Boujaoude, S., Duschl, R., Lederman, N., Mamlok-Naaman, R., Hofstein, A., et al. (2004). Inquiry in science education: International perspectives. *Science Education, 88,* 397–419.

Akerson, V. L., & Young, T. A. (2005). Science the "write" way. *Science and Children, 43*(3), 38–41.

Almasi, J. (2002). *Teaching strategic processes in reading.* New York: Guilford Press.

Alvermann, D., & Moore, D. (1991). Secondary school reading. In R. Barr, M. Kamil, P. Mosenthal, & P. D. Pearson (Eds.), *Handbook of reading research* (Vol. II, pp. 951–983). New York: Longman.

Alvermann, D., Phelps, S., & Gillis, V. (2010). *Content area reading and literacy: Succeeding in today's diverse classroom* (6th ed.). Boston, MA: Allyn & Bacon.

American Association for the Advancement of Science. (1993). *Benchmarks for science literacy.* New York: Oxford University Press.

Anderson, R. (2004). Role of the reader's schema in comprehension, learning, and memory. In R. Ruddell & N. Unrau (Eds.), *Theoretical models and processes of reading* (5th ed., pp. 594–606). Newark, DE: International Reading Association.

Anderson, R. D. (2002). Reforming science teaching: What research says about inquiry. *Journal of Research in Science Teaching, 13*(1), 1–12.

Barnitz, J. G. (1998). Revising grammar instruction for authentic composing and comprehending. *The Reading Teacher, 51*(7), 608–611.

Bean, T. W., Readence, J. E., & Baldwin, R. S. (2008). *Content area literacy: An integrated approach* (9th ed.). Dubuque, IA: Kendall Hunt Publishing.

Beck, I., McKeown, M., Hamilton, R., & Kucan, L. (1997). *Questioning the author: An approach for enhancing student engagement with text.* Newark, DE: International Reading Association.

Beck, I., McKeown, M., Sandora, C., Kucan, L., & Worthy, J. (1996). Questioning the author: A yearlong classroom implementation to engage students with text. *The Elementary School Journal, 96,* 385–414.

Beers, K. (2002). *When kids can't read, what teachers can do: A guide for teachers 6–12.* Portsmouth, NH: Heinemann.

Bell, R. L., Smetana, L., & Binns, I. (2005). Simplifying inquiry instruction. *The Science Teacher, 72*(7), 30–33.

Bereiter, C., & Scardamalia, M. (1987). *The psychology of written communication*. Hillsdale, NJ: Lawrence Erlbaum.

Biancarosa, G., & Snow, C. (2004). *Reading next—A vision for action and research in middle and high school literacy: A report from Carnegie Corporation of New York*. Washington, DC: Alliance for Excellent Education.

Brown, R., Pressley, M., van Meter, P., & Schuder, T. (2004). A quasi-experimental validation of transactional strategies instruction with low-achieving second-grade readers. In R. Ruddell & N. Unrau (Eds.), *Theoretical models and processes of reading* (5th ed., pp. 998–1039). Newark, DE: International Reading Association.

Bruning, R., & Horn, C. (2000). Developing motivation to write. *Educational Psychologists, 35*(1), 25–37.

Bunce, D. M. (2002). *Inquiry learning: What is it and how do you do it?* Washington, DC: American Chemical Society.

Bybee, R. W., Powell, J. C., & Trowbridge, L. W. (2007). *Teaching secondary school science: Strategies for developing scientific literacy*. Upper Saddle River, NJ: Prentice Hall.

Calkins, L. (2004). *The art of teaching writing*. Portsmouth, NH: Heinemann.

Cervetti, G., & Barber, J. (2009). Bringing back books: Using text to support hands-on investigations for scientific inquiry. *Science and Children, 47*(3), 36–39.

Cervetti, G., Pearson, P. D., Bravo, M. A., & Barber, J. (2006). Reading and writing in the service of inquiry-based science. In R. Douglas, M. Klentschy, & K. Worth (Eds.), *Linking science and literacy in the K–8 classroom* (pp. 221–244). Arlington, VA: The National Science Teachers Association.

Chall, J., Jacobs, V., & Baldwin, L. (1990). *The reading crisis: Why poor children fall behind*. Cambridge, MA: Harvard University Press.

Chang, C. Y., & Mao, S. L. (1999). Comparison of Taiwan science students' outcomes with inquiry-group versus traditional instruction. *Journal of Educational Research, 92*(6), 340–349.

Chiappetta, E. L., & Adams, A. D. (2004). Inquiry-based instruction. *The Science Teacher, 71*(2), 46–50.

Christie, F., & Derewianka, B. (2008). *School discourse: Learning to write across the year of schooling*. London: Continuum.

Colburn, A. (2008). *What teacher educators need to know about inquiry-based instruction*. Retrieved March 10, 2010, from http://www.csulb.edu/~acolburn/AETS.htm.

Craig, M., & Yore, L. (1995). Middle school students' metacognitive knowledge about science reading and science text: An interview study. *Reading Psychology, 16*, 169–213.

Crawford, B. A. (2000). Embracing the essence of inquiry: New roles for science teachers. *Journal of Research in Science Teaching, 37*(9), 916–937.

Crawford, B. A. (2007). Learning to teach science as inquiry in the rough and tumble of practice. *Journal of Research in Science Teaching, 44*(4), 613–642.

Creech, J., & Hale, G. (2006). Literacy in science: A natural fit. *The Science Teacher, 73*(2), 22–27.

Dalton, B., Morocco, C., Tivnan, T., & Mead, P. (1997). Supported inquiry science: Teaching for conceptual change in urban and suburban science classrooms. *Journal of Learning Disabilities, 30*, 670–684.

Daniels, H. (1994). *Literature circles: Voice and choice in book clubs and reading groups.* Portland, ME: Stenhouse.

Derewianka, B. (1990). *Exploring how texts work.* Maryborough, Victoria, Australia: Primary English Teaching Association.

Dlugokienski, A., & Sampson, V. (2008). Learning to write and writing to learn in science: Refutational texts and analytical rubrics. *Science Scope, 32*(3), 14–19.

Dole, J., & Smith, E. J. (1989). Prior knowledge and learning from science text: An instructional study. *National Reading Conference Yearbook, 38,* 345–352. Chicago: National Reading Conference.

Duit, R. (1991). On the role of analogies and metaphors in learning science. *Science Education, 75*(6), 649–672.

Duke, N. (2000). 3.6 minutes per day: The scarcity of informational texts in first grade. *Reading Research Quarterly, 35*(2), 202–225.

Duke, N. (2004). The case for informational text. *Educational Leadership, 61*(6), 40–44.

Duplichan, S. C. (2009). Using web logs in the science classroom. *Science Scope, 33*(1), 33–37.

Fang, Z. (2002). The construction of literate understanding in a literature-based classroom. *Journal of Research in Reading, 25*(1), 109–126.

Fang, Z. (2005). Scientific literacy: A systemic functional linguistics perspective. *Science Education, 89,* 335–347.

Fang, Z. (2006). The language demands of science reading in middle school. *International Journal of Science Education, 28,* 491–520.

Fang, Z. (2008). Going beyond the 'Fab Five': Helping students cope with the unique challenges of expository reading in intermediate grades. *Journal of Adolescent and Adult Literacy, 51*(6), 476–487.

Fang, Z. (in press). The challenges of reading disciplinary texts. In C. Shanahan & T. Shanahan (Eds.), *Adolescent literacy within the disciplines: General principles and practical strategies.* New York: Guilford.

Fang, Z., Lamme, L., Pringle, R., Patrick, J., Sanders, J., Zmach, C., et al. (2008). Integrating reading into middle school science: What we did, found and learned. *International Journal of Science Education, 30*(15), 2067–2089.

Fang, Z., & Schleppegrell, M. J. (2008). *Reading in secondary content areas: A language-based pedagogy.* Ann Arbor: University of Michigan Press.

Fang, Z., & Schleppegrell, M. J. (2010). Disciplinary literacies across content areas: Supporting secondary reading through functional language analysis. *Journal of Adolescent and Adult Literacy, 53*(7), 587–597.

Fang, Z., Schleppegrell, M. J., & Cox, B. E. (2006). Understanding the language demands of schooling: Nouns in academic registers. *Journal of Literacy Research, 38*(3), 247–273.

Fang, Z., & Wang, Z. (in press). Beyond rubrics: Using functional language analysis to evaluate student writing. *Australian Journal of Language and Literacy.*

Fang, Z., & Wei, Y. (2010). Improving middle school students' science literacy through reading infusion. *Journal of Educational Research, 103*(4), 262–273.

Fay, M. E., & Bretz, S. L. (2008). Structuring the level of inquiry in your classroom. *The Science Teacher, 75*(5), 38–42.

Fellows, N. J. (1994). A window into thinking: Using student writing to understand conceptual change in science learning. *Journal of Research in Science Teaching, 31*(9), 985–1001.

Fisher, D., Brozo, W. G., Frey, N., & Ivey, G. (2011). *50 instructional routines to develop content literacy* (2nd ed.). Boston: Pearson.

Gaskins, I., Guthrie, J., Satlow, E., Ostertag, J., Six, L., Byrne, J., et al. (1994). Integrating instruction of science, reading, and writing: Goals, teacher development, and assessment. *Journal of Research in Science Teaching, 31*(9), 1039–1056.

Gee, J. (2001). Reading as situated language: A sociocognitive perspective. *Journal of Adolescent and Adult Literacy, 44*, 714–725.

Glynn, S. M., Duit, R., & Thiele, R. B. (1995). Teaching science with analogies: A strategy for constructing knowledge. In S. M. Glynn & R. Duit (Eds.). *Learning science in the schools: Research reforming practice* (pp. 247–273). Mahwah, NJ: Lawrence Erlbaum.

Glynn, S. M., & Muth, K. D. (1994). Reading and writing to learn science: Achieving scientific literacy. *Journal of Research in Science Teaching, 31*, 1057–1073.

Gonzales, P., Williams, T., Jocelyn, L., Roey, S., Kastberg, D., & Brenwald, S. (2008). *Highlights from TIMSS 2007: Mathematics and science achievement of U.S. fourth- and eighth-grade students in an international context.* Washington, DC: U.S. Department of Education.

Griffin, C., Simmons, D., & Kameenui, E. (1991). Investigating the effectiveness of graphic organizer instruction on the comprehension and recall of science content by students with learning disabilities. *Reading, Writing, and Learning Disabilities, 7*, 355–376.

Grigg, W., Lauko, M., & Brockway, D. (2006). *The nation's report card: Science 2005 assessment of student performance in grades 4, 8 and 12* (NCES 2006466). Washington, DC: National Center for Educational Statistics.

Guthrie, J., Van Meter, P., Hancock, G., Alao, S., Anderson, E., & McCann, A. (1998). Does concept-oriented reading instruction increase strategy use and conceptual learning from text? *Journal of Educational Psychology, 90*, 261–278.

Guzzetti, B., Snyder, T., Glass, G., & Gamas, W. (1993). Promoting conceptual change in science: Meta-analysis of instructional interventions from reading education and science education. *Reading Research Quarterly, 28*, 116–161.

Hadaway, N. L., Vardell, S. M., & Young, T. A. (2001). Scaffolding oral language development through poetry for students learning English. *The Reading Teacher, 54*, 796–806.

Haggard, M. R. (1986). The vocabulary self-collection strategy: Using student interest and world knowledge to enhance vocabulary growth. *Journal of Reading, 29*(7), 634–642.

Halliday, M. A. K. (1994). *An introduction to functional grammar* (2nd ed.). London: Edward Arnold.

Halliday, M. A. K. (1998). Things and relations: Regrammaticising experience as technical knowledge. In J. R. Martin & R. Veel (Eds.), *Reading science: Critical and functional perspectives on discourses of science* (pp. 185–235). London: Routledge.

Halliday, M. A. K., & Martin, J. R. (1993). *Writing science: Literacy and discursive power.* Pittsburgh, PA: University of Pittsburgh Press.

Halliday, M. A. K., & Matthiessen, C. (2004). *An introduction to functional grammar* (3rd ed.). London: Arnold.

Hand, B., Alvermann, D., Gee, J., Guzzetti, B., Norris, S., & Phillips, L., et al. (2003). Guest editorial: Message from the "Island Group": What is literacy in science literacy? *Journal of Research in Science Teaching, 40*(7), 607–615.

Hand, B., & Key, C. (1999). Inquiry investigation. *The Science Teacher, 66*(4), 27–29.

Hand, B., Prain, V., Lawrence, C., & Yore, L. (1999). A writing in science framework designed to enhance science literacy. *International Journal of Science Education, 21*(19), 1021–1035.

Harvey, S., & Goudvis, A. (2007). *Strategies that work: Teaching comprehension for understanding and engagement* (2nd ed.). Portland, ME: Stenhouse.

Hildebrand, G. M. (1998). Disrupting hegemonic writing practices in school science: Contesting the right way to write. *Journal of Research in Science Teaching, 35*, 345–362.

Hirsch, E. D., Jr. (2006). *The knowledge deficit: Closing the shocking education gap for American children.* Boston: Houghton Mifflin.

Hmelo-Silver, C. E., Duncan, R. G., & Chin, C. A. (2007). Scaffolding and achievement in problem-based and inquiry learning: A response to Kirschner, Sweller, and Clark (2006). *Educational Psychologist, 42*, 99–107.

Hohenshell, L. M., & Hand, B. (2006). Writing-to-learn strategies in secondary school cell biology: A mixed method study. *International Journal of Science Education, 28*(2–3), 261–289.

Hudson, S. B., McMahon, K. C., Overstreet, C. M. (2002). *The 2000 national survey of science and mathematics education: Compendium of tables.* Chapel Hill, NC: Horizon Research.

Ivey, G., & Broaddus, K. (2001). "Just plain reading": A survey of what makes students want to read in middle school classrooms. *Reading Research Quarterly, 36*, 350–377.

Jones, L. (2006, October). *How textbooks influence the formal EE curriculum: A case study.* Paper presented at the annual meeting of North American Association for Environmental Education, Minneapolis, Minnesota.

Kamil, M., & Bernhardt, E. (2004). The science of reading and the reading of science: Successes, failures, and promises in the search for prerequisite reading skills for science. In W. Saul (Ed.), *Crossing borders in literacy and science instruction: Perspectives on theory and practice* (pp. 123–139). Newark, DE: International Reading Association.

Keene, E. O., & Zimmermann, S. (2007). *Mosaic of thought: The power of comprehension strategy instruction* (2nd ed.). Portsmouth, NH: Heinemann.

Key, C. W., Hand, B., Prain, V., & Collins, S. (1999). Using the science writing heuristic as a tool for learning from laboratory investigations in secondary science. *Journal of Research in Science Teaching, 36*(10), 1065–1084.

King, R. (1990). Poetry and science in the classroom. *Insights into Open Education, 22*(5). (ERIC Document Reproduction Service No. ED313716).

Kintsch, W. (2004). The construction-integration model of text comprehension and its implications for instruction. In R. Ruddell & N. Unrau (Eds.), *Theoretical models and processes of reading* (5th ed., pp. 1270–1328). Newark, DE: International Reading Association.

Klentschy, M. (2005). Science notebook essentials. *Science and Children, 43*(30), 24–27.

Kress, G. (2003). Genres and the multimodal production of "scientificness." In G. Kress & C. Jewitt (Eds.), *Multimodal literacy* (pp. 173–186). New York: Peter Lang.

Kress, G., Jewitt, C., Ogborn, J., & Tsatsarelis, C. (2001). *Multimodal teaching and learning: The rhetorics of the science classroom.* London: Continuum.

Lemke, J. (1989). Making text talk. *Theory into Practice, 28,* 136–141.

Lemke, J. (1998). Multiplying meaning: Visual and verbal semiotics in scientific text. In J. Martin & R. Veel (Eds.), *Reading science: Critical and functional perspectives on discourses of science* (pp. 87–113). New York: Routledge.

Lemke, J. (2000). Multimedia literacy demands of the scientific curriculum. *Linguistics and Education, 10,* 247–271.

Lemke, J. (2001). Foreword. In J. Wellington & J. Osborne, *Language and literacy in science education* (pp. iv–v). Philadelphia: Open University Press.

Lemke, J. (2002). Multimedia semiotics: Genres for science education and scientific literacy. In M. J. Schleppegrell & M. C. Colombi (Eds.), *Developing advanced literacy in first and second languages: Meaning with power* (pp. 21–44). Mahwah, NJ: Lawrence Erlbaum.

Lyman, F. T. (1981). The responsive classroom discussion. The inclusion of all students. In A. Anderson (Ed.), *Mainstreaming digest* (pp. 109–113). College Park: The University of Maryland Press.

Martin, J. R. (1989). *Factual writing: Exploring and challenging the experiential world.* Oxford, England: Oxford University Press.

Martin, J. R. & Veel, R. (1998). *Reading science: Critical and functional perspectives on discourses of science.* New York: Routledge.

Mason, L., & Boscolo, P. (2000). Writing and conceptual change: What changes? *Instructional Science, 28*(3), 199–226.

McDermott, M. (2010). Using multimodal writing tasks in science classrooms. *The Science Teacher, 77* 32–36.

McDonald, J., & Domingez, L. (2009). Reflective writing. *The Science Teacher, 76*(3), 46–49.

Mesa, J., Klosterman, M., & Jones, L. (2008). The P.O.E.T.R.Y. of science: A flexible tool for assessing elementary student science journals. *Science and Children, 46*(3), 36–41.

Minstrell, J., & van Zee, E. H. (2000). *Inquiring into inquiry learning and teaching in science.* Washington, DC: American Association for the Advancement of Science.

Monhardt, R. (2005). Reading & writing nonfiction with children: Using biographies to learn about science and scientists. *Science and Children, 28*(6), 16–19.

Morrow, L., Pressley, M., Smith, J., & Smith, M. (1997). The effect of a literature-based program integrated into literacy and science instruction with children from diverse backgrounds. *Reading Research Quarterly, 32,* 54–76.

Moss, B. (2008). The information text gap: The mismatch between non-narrative text types in basal readers and 2009 NAEP recommended guidelines. *Journal of Literacy Research, 40*(2), 201–219.

Moss, B., & Newton, E. (2002). An examination of the informational text genre in basal readers. *Reading Psychology, 23*(1), 1–13.

Myhill, D. (2009). Becoming a designer: Trajectories of linguistic development. In R. Beard, D. Myhill, J. Riley, & M. Nystrand (Eds.), *The Sage handbook of writing development* (pp. 402–414). London: Sage Publications.

National Reading Panel. (2000). *Teaching children to read: An evidence-based assessment of the scientific research literature on reading and its implications for reading instruction.* Washington, DC: National Institute of Child Health and Human Development.

National Research Council. (1996). *National science education standards.* Washington, DC: National Academy Press.

National Research Council. (2000). *Inquiry and the national science education standards: A guide for teaching and learning.* Washington, DC: National Academy Press.

National Science Foundation. (1999). *Inquiry: Thoughts, views and strategies for the K–5 classroom* (Foundations, Vol. 2). Arlington, VA: National Science Foundation.

Norris, S., & Phillips, L. (2003). How literacy in its fundamental sense is central to scientific literacy. *Science Education, 87*(2), 224–240.

Novak, J. D. (1998). *Learning, creating, and using knowledge: Concept maps as facilitative tools in schools and corporations.* Mahwah, NJ: Lawrence Erlbaum.

Ogle, D. (1986). K-W-L: A teaching model that develops active reading of expository text. *The Reading Teacher, 39,* 564–570.

O'Halloran, K. L. (Ed.) (2004). *Multimodal discourse analysis: Systemic functional perspectives.* London: Continuum.

O'Halloran, K. L. (2005). *Mathematical discourse: Language, symbolism and visual images.* London: Continuum.

Orgill, M., & Thomas, M. (2007). Analogies and the 5E model. *The Science Teacher, 74*(1), 40–45.

Osborne, J., Simon, S., & Collins, S. (2003). Attitudes towards science: A review of the literature and its implications. *International Journal of Science Education, 25,* 1049–1079.

Palinscar, A., & Brown, A. (1984). Reciprocal teaching of comprehension fostering and comprehension monitoring activities. *Cognition and Instruction, 1,* 117–176.

Palinscar, A., & Magnusson, S. J. (2001). The interplay of firsthand and text-based investigations to model and support the development of scientific knowledge and reasoning. In S. Carver & D. Glahr (Eds.), *Cognition and instruction: Twenty-five years of progress* (pp. 151–194). Mahwah, NJ: Lawrence Erlbaum.

Palmatier, R. (1973). A note taking system for learning. *Journal of Reading, 17,* 36–39.

Pehrsson, R. S., & Robinson, H. A. (1985). *The semantic organizer approach to writing and reading instruction.* Rockville, MD: Aspen Systems Corporation.

Perera, K. (2005). The 'good book': Linguistic aspects. In Z. Fang (Ed.), *Literacy teaching and learning: Current issues and trends* (pp. 134–143). Columbus, OH: Merrill.

Perie, M., Grigg, W., & Donahue, P. (2005). *The nation's report card: Reading 2005* (NCES, 2006451). Washington, DC: National Center for Educational Statistics.

Prain, V. (2006). Learning from writing in secondary science: Some theoretical and practical implications. *International Journal of Science Education, 28*(2–3), 179–201.

Prain, V., & Hand, B. (1996). Writing for learning in secondary science: Rethinking practices. *Teaching & Teacher Education, 12*(6), 609–626.

Prain, V., & Waldrip, B. (Eds.) (2010). Special Issue: Representing science literacies. *Research in Science Education, 40*(1).

Pressley, M. (2004). The need for research on secondary literacy instruction. In T. L. Jetton & J. A. Dole (Eds.), *Adolescent literacy research and practice* (pp. 415–432). New York: Guilford.

RAND Reading Study Group. (2002). *Reading for understanding: Toward a RAND program in reading comprehension.* Santa Monica, CA: RAND Corporation.

Reif, F., & Larkin, J. (1991). Cognition in scientific and everyday domains: Comparison and learning implications. *Journal of Research in Science Teaching, 28*(9), 733–760.

Resnick, L. B. (1987). *Education and learning to think.* Washington, DC: National Academy Press.

Rivard, L. P. (1994). A review of writing to learn in science: Implications for practice and research. *Journal of Research in Science Teaching, 31*(9), 969–983.

Rivard, L. P., & Straw, S. B. (2000). The effect of talk and writing on learning science: An exploratory study. *Science Education, 84,* 566–593.

Robertson, A., & Mahlin, K. (2005). Ecosystem journalism. *Science and Children, 43*(3), 42–45.

Robertson, B. (2005). What writing represents what scientists actually do? *Science and Children, 43*(3), 50–51.

Robinson, F. (1946). *Effective study.* New York: Harper & Row.

Robinson, P. J. (2005). Teaching key vocabulary in geography and science classrooms: An analysis of teachers' practice with particular reference to EAL pupils' learning. *Language and Education, 19*(5), 428–445.

Romance, N., & Vitale, M. (1992). A curriculum strategy that expands time for in-depth elementary science instruction by using science-based reading strategies: Effects of a year-long study in grade 4. *Journal of Research in Science Teaching, 63,* 201–243.

Rutherford, F. J., & Ahlgren, A. (1990). *Science for all Americans.* New York: Oxford University Press.

Saul, E. W. (2004). *Crossing borders in literacy and science instruction: Perspectives on theory into practice.* Newark, DE: International Reading Association.

Schleppegrell, M. J. (2004). *The language of schooling: A functional linguistics perspective.* Mahwah, NJ: Lawrence Erlbaum.

Schleppegrell, M. J., & Colombi, M. C. (1997). Text organization by bilingual writers: Clause structure as a reflection of discourse structure. *Written Communication, 14*(4), 481–503.

Schleppegrell, M. J., Greer, S., & Taylor, S. (2008). Literacy in history: Language and meaning. *Australian Journal of Language and Literacy, 31*(2), 174–187.

Schwartz, R., & Raphael, T. (1985). Concept of definition: A key to improving students' vocabulary. *Reading Teacher, 39,* 198–203.

Shymansky, J. A., Kyle, W. C., Jr., & Alport, J. M. (1983). The effects of new science curricular on student performance. *Journal of Research in Science Teaching, 20*(5), 387–404.

Smith, F. (1996). *Reading without nonsense* (3rd ed.). New York: Teachers College Press.

Straits, W. (2005). Mystery box writing. *Science and Children, 43*(3), 33–37.

Straits, W. (2007). Literature-circles approach to understanding science as a human endeavor. *Science Scope, 31*(2), 32–36.

Straits, W., & Nichols, S. (2006). Literature circles for science. *Science and Children, 44*(3), 52–55.

Tompkins, G. E. (2009). *50 literacy strategies.* Boston: Allyn & Bacon.

Turner, T., & Broemmel, A. (2006). 14 writing strategies. *Science Scope, 30*(4), 27–31.

Unsworth, L. (1997a). Scaffolding reading of science explanations: Assessing the grammatical and visual forms of specialized knowledge. *Reading, 31*(3), 30–42.

Unsworth, L. (1997b). Some practicalities of a language-based theory of learning. *Australian Journal of Language and Literacy, 20,* 36–52.

Unsworth, L. (2001). *Teaching multiliteracies across the curriculum: Changing contexts of text and image in classroom practice.* Philadelphia: Open University Press.

Vacca, R. T., Vacca, J. A. L., & Mraz, M. (2011). *Content area reading: Literacy and learning across the curriculum* (10th ed.). Boston: Pearson.

Veel, R. (1997). Learning how to mean—scientifically speaking: Apprenticeship into scientific discourse in the secondary school. In F. Christie & J. R. Martin (Eds.), *Genre and institutions: Social processes in the workplace and school* (pp. 161–195). London: Cassell.

Veel, R., & Coffin, C. (1996). Learning to think like an historian: The language of secondary school history. In R. Hasan & G. Williams (Eds.), *Literacy in society* (pp. 191–231). London: Longman.

Wade, S., & Moje, E. (2000). The role of text in classroom learning. In M. Kamil, P. Mosenthal, P. D. Pearson, & R. Barr (Eds.), *Handbook of reading research* (Vol. III, pp. 609–627). Mahwah, NJ: Lawrence Erlbaum.

Warwick, P., Stephenson, P., & Webster, J. (2003). Developing pupils' written expression of procedural understanding through the use of writing frames in science: Findings from a case study approach. *International Journal of Science Education, 25*(2), 173–192.

Weiss, I. R., Pasley, J. D., Smith, P. S., Banilower, E. R., & Heck, D. J. (2003). *Looking inside the classroom: A study of K–12 mathematics and science education in the U.S.* Chapel Hill, NC: Horizon Research.

Wellington, J., & Osborne, J. (2001). *Language and literacy in science education.* Philadelphia: Open University Press.

Wilson, C. D., Taylor, J. A., Kowalski, S. M., & Carlson, J. (2010). The relative effects and equity of inquiry-based and commonplace science teaching on students' knowledge, reasoning, and argumentation. *Journal of Research in Science Teaching, 47*(3), 276–301.

Wise, K. C., & Okey, J. R. (1983). A meta-analysis of the effects of various science teaching strategies on achievement. *Journal of Research in Science Teaching, 20*(5), 419–435.

Yager, R. E. (2004). Science is not written, but it can be written about. In W. E. Saul (Ed.), *Crossing borders in literacy and science instruction: Perspectives on theory and practice* (pp. 95–108). Arlington, VA: NSTA Press and Newark, DE: IRA.

Young, T. A., Moss, B., & Cornwell, L. (2007). The classroom library: A place for nonfiction, nonfiction in its place. *Reading Horizons, 48*(1), 1–18.

Yore, L., Bisanz, G., & Hand, B. M. (2003). Examining the literacy component of science literacy: 25 years of language and science research. *International Journal of Science Education, 25*(6), 689–725.

Yore, L. D., Hand, B. M., & Florence, M. K. (2004). Scientists' views of science, models of writing, and science writing practices. *Journal of Research in Science Teaching, 41*(4), 338–369.

Yore, L. D., Hand, B. M., Goldman, S., Hildebrand, G., Osborne, J., Treagust, D., et al. (2004). New directions in language and science education research. *Reading Research Quarterly, 39*(3), 347–352.

Yore, L., Hand, B., & Prain, V. (2002). Scientists as writers. *Science Education, 86*, 672–692.

Yore, L., & Treagust, D. (2006). Current realities and future possibilities: Language and science literacy—empowering research and informing instruction. *International Journal of Science Education, 28*(2–3), 291–314.

Zales, C. R., & Unger, C. S. (2008). The science and literacy framework. *Science and Children, 46*(3), 42–45.

Children's Books Cited

Baldwin, C. (2004). *Acids and bases.* Chicago: Raintree.

Bedini, S. (1984). *The life of Benjamin Banneker.* Rancho Cordova, CA: Landmark Enterprises.

Brown, M. (2004). *The world of Arthur and friends: Six Arthur adventures in one volume.* New York: Little, Brown and Company.

Catherall, E. (1990). *Exploring electricity.* Austin, TX: Steck-Vaughn.

Chasek, R. (2000). *Rocks and minerals.* New York: Grolier Publishing.

Ellyard, D. (1996). *Weather.* San Francisco: Time Life Books.

Flanagan, A. K. (2000). *Rocks.* Minneapolis, MN: Compass Point Books.

Frisch, J. (2003). *Temperature: Understanding science.* North Mankato, MN: Smart Apple Media.

Gallant, R. A. (1998). *Limestone.* Danbury, CT: Grolier Publishing.

Glencoe/McGraw-Hill. (2000a). *Science voyages: Exploring the life, earth, and physical sciences* (Red level, Florida edition). Columbus, OH: Author.

Glencoe/McGraw-Hill. (2000b). *Science voyages: Exploring the life, earth, and physical sciences* (Green level, Florida edition). Columbus, OH: Author.

Horenstein, S. (1993). *Rocks tell stories.* Brookfield, CT: The Millbrook Presss.

Johnson, R. L. (2004). *Acids and bases.* Washington, DC: National Geographic Society.

Kittinger, J. S. (1997). *A look at rocks: From coal to kimberlite.* New York: Franklin Watts.

Lambert, D. (1997). *The Kingfisher young people's book of ocean.* New York: Kingfisher.

Miller, G. T. (2004). *Living in the environment: Principles, connections, and solutions* (13th ed.). Pacific Grove, CA: Brooks/Cole.

Murphy, J. (2003). *An American plague: The true and terrifying story of the yellow fever epidemic of 1793.* New York: Clarion Books.

Oldfield, S. (2002). *Rainforest.* Cambridge, MA: The MIT Press.

Oxlade, C. (2002). *Elements and compounds.* Chicago: Heinemann Library.

Oxlade, C. (2007). *Acids and bases: Chemicals in action.* Oxford, England: Heinemann Library.

Parker, S. (1992). *Electricity.* New York: Dorling Kindersley.

Piddock, C. (2008). *Outbreak: Science seeks safeguards for global health.* Washington, DC: National Geographic Society.

Pobst, S. (2008). *Animals on the edge: Science races to save species threatened with extinction.* Washington, DC: National Geographic Society.

Sands, S. (2006a). *Kids Discover: Grand Canyon.* New York: Kids Discover.

Sands, S. (2006b). *Kids Discover: Insects.* New York: Kids Discover.

Sands, S. (2006c). *Kids Discover: Planets.* New York: Kids Discover.

Sands, S. (2006d). *Kids Discover: Plants.* New York: Kids Discover.

Scott Foresman. (2000). *Science Grade 5.* New York: Scott Foresman.

Symes, R. F. (2004). *Rocks and minderals.* New York: DK Publishing.

Urban, L. (2007). *A crooked kind of perfect.* Orlando, FL: Harcourt.

Walker, R. (2003). *Genes and DNA.* Boston: Kingfisher.

Zim, H. S., & Shaffer, P. R. (1985). Rocks and minerals: A guide to familiar minerals, gems, ores and rocks. New York: Golden Books.

Index

Abstraction, 23–25
Academic research report, 105
Adjectives, 24, 25
Adverbs, 25
Affixes, 52
American Association for the
    Advancement of Science
    (AAAS), 2, 37
    lifetime achievement award, 46
American Library Association (ALA),
    37, 44–45
Analogy analysis, 123–124
Anticipation guide, 81–83
Aristotle, 52
Arnold, C., 47
Arnosky, J., 46, 47
Articles, 25
Artist science writers, 46
Asimov, I., 47
Association for Library Service to
    Children (ALSC), 37
Audience for writing, 112
Author information, 38
    bibliographies and source notes,
        40–41
    questioning-the-author strategy, 88–90
    science author studies, 46–47
Auxiliary verbs, 25
Award-winning trade books, 36–37

Background knowledge and text
    comprehension, 21–22, 34
Benchmarks for Scientific Literacy, 2
Bibliography, 40–41
Biographers of scientists, 46
Biographical literature about scientists,
    42–43, 120–121
Biographical profiles of authors and
    artists, 38

Biography book projects, 120–121
Book Links, 44–45
Book study groups, 45–46
Broemmel, A., 127
Brown, R., 78
Burnie, D., 46

Captions, 40
Carlson, J., 4
Chang, C. Y., 5
Charts, 40
Children's Book Council, 36–37
Chin, C. A., 5
Classifier, 61
Class publications, 119–120
Clauses, 25–28, 30–31, 71–72, 129
Coffin, C., 76
Cognitive and metacognitive skills, 77
Collard III, S. B., 47
Comprehension. *See* Text
    comprehension
Concept definition word map, 57–59, 113
Concept mapping, 125
Conjunctions, 25, 69–71
Connectives, 69–71
Constructivism, 3, 111–112
Content knowledge in science, 34
Cooperative learning strategy, reciprocal
    teaching, 90–92
Coordinate clause, 26, 129
Crawford, B., 8
Crick, F., 71
Critical reading:
    checking sources, 41
    Questioning-the-author strategy,
        88–90
    using author biographical
        information, 42
Cultural model, 20

Dalton, B., 5
Davies, N., 46
Deem, J. M., 46
Definition game, 66–68
Delano, M. F., 46
Demonstratives, 25
Dendy, L., 46
Derewianka, B., 49–50
Describer, 61
Descriptive report, 106
Dominguez, L., 116
Duke, N., 49
Duncan, R. G., 5
Duplichan, S., 117

Elaboration tasks, 63
Embedded clause, 26, 28–29, 62–63,
    71–72
E-pal projects, 122–123
Explanation text, 106
Exposition text, 106
Expository science language, student
    exposure to, 49–50

Fair testing, 8
Fang, Z., 46
Farrell, J., 46

Gee, J., 20
Genre, 112
George, J. C., 47
Genre teaching cycle, 110–111
Glossary, 39
Grammatical items, 25
Graphic organizer, 92–94
Graphs, 40, 118

Haggard, M., 59
Halliday, M. A. K., 28
Halls, K. M., 46
Hand, B., 104, 111, 115, 125
Harris, J., 46
Heuristic for science writing, 124–125
Hmelo-Silver, C. E., 5
Hoose, P., 46
Hopping, L. J., 46

Illustrations, 38, 39–40, 118
Impersonal authoritativeness, 31–32
Independent reading, 51
Index, 39
Informational storybooks, 51. *See also*
    Science trade books
Informational density, 25–30

Inquiry-based science, 2–3
    activity-based science, 5
    benefits of, 3–5
    essential features of, 6–8
    incorporating into classroom
        practice, 5–9
    language and literacy in, 14–16
    levels of inquiry, 9
    National Science Education Standards,
        2, 3, 4, 6
    sample lessons, 9–14
    supported inquiry science, 5
Interactive-constructivist model,
    111–112
International comparisons in mathematics
    and science achievement, 1
Internet safety issues, 117

Journals, 115–116

King, R., 43
Klentschy, M., 115
Kowalski, S. M., 4
Kress, G., 33
Krull, K., 46
Kunkel, D., 40
KWL, 13, 83–85

Lab activities, science writing heuristic,
    124–125
Language and literacy in inquiry-based
    science, 14–16. *See also* Science
    reading; Text comprehension
Language-based tasks, 51, 77
    definition game, 66–68
    developing awareness about textual
        signposts, 69–71
    learning about nouns, 61–69
    paraphrasing, 73–75
    syntactic anatomy and integration,
        71–73
    theory and evidence base, 76
    vocabulary development, 52–61
    See also Nouns; Vocabulary
Language of science, 51
    linguistic challenges, 22–32
    student exposure to, 49–50
    See also Language-based tasks;
        Science grammar
Lauber, P., 46, 47
Lawrence, C., 125
Learning logs, 116–117
Lemke, J., 2, 33
Lexical density, 25–30

Lexical items, 25
Lifetime achievement award, 46
Lindop, L., 46
Linguistic knowledge and text
    comprehension, 21–22
    abstraction, 23–25
    density, 25–30
    impersonal authoritativeness, 31–32
    metaphorical realizations of logical
        reasoning, 30–31
    technicality, 23
Linnaeus, C., 52
Literature circles, 45
Logical reasoning, 30–31
Long nouns, 29–30
    deconstruction, 61–63

Macaulay, D., 47
Mahlin, K., 119
Main clause, 26
Mao, S. L., 5
Maps, 40
Markle, S., 46
Martin, J., 110
Mason, A., 46
McDermott, M., 118
McDonald, J., 116
Mead, P., 5
Mealworms, 113–114
Metaphorical realizations of logical
    reasoning, 30–31
Method of text production, 112
Miller, D. S., 46
Miller, R., 46
Monhardt, R., 120
Montgomery, S., 46, 47
Morocco, C., 5
Morphemic analysis, 52–56
Multimodal and multisemiotic texts, 33
Multimodal writing projects, 118–119
Murphy, J., 47
Mystery Box Writing, 122

National Assessment of Educational
    Progress (NAEP), 1, 16
National Council of Teachers of English
    (NCTE), 37
National Research Council (NRC), 2
National Science Content Standards,
    36–37
National Science Education Standards,
    2, 3, 4, 6
National Science Teachers Association
    (NSTA), 36–37

National Wildlife Federation (NWF),
    40–41
Nichols, S., 41
Nominalization, 24–25, 68–69
Norris, S., 15
Note taking strategy, 96–97, 101–102
Nouns, 25, 61
    abstraction, 23–25
    definition game, 66–68
    deconstruction, 61–63
    expansion, 63
    head, 28, 29, 61, 62
    long nouns, 29–30, 61–63
    nominalization, 24–25, 68–69
    noun search activity, 63–66
    sentence completion activity, 68–69
NSTA Outstanding Science Trade
    Books for Students K–12, 36
Numerative, 61

Ogle, D., 83
O'Halloran, K., 33
Orbis Pictus Award for Outstanding
    Nonfiction for Children, 37
Organizing information, using graphic
    organizer, 92–94
Osborne, J., 15, 49, 78, 127

Paraphrasing, 73–75
Passive voice, 31
Patent, D. H., 46, 47
Phillips, L., 15
Platt, R., 46
Poetry studies, 43
Pointer, 61
Positive environments for writing to
    learn, 112
Postmodifiers, 62
PowerPoint, 51
Prain, V., 33, 104, 111, 115, 125
Prefixes 52, 53
Premodifiers, 61
Prepositions, 25
Prepositional phrases, 28, 62, 73
Pressley, M., 78
Pringle, L., 46, 47
Prior knowledge, 81
    Anticipation guide, 81–83
    KWL strategy, 83–85
    PKMI, 85–86
Prior knowledge monitoring and
    integration (PKMI), 85–86
Procedural recount, 106
Procedural text, 105

Pronouns, 25
Purpose for writing, 112

Qualifiers, 62
Questioning the author (QTA), 88–90
Quickwrites, 126

Raconteurs of science, 127
Raphael, T., 58
Reading aloud, 44–45
Reading and active sense making, 86
Reading and writing and inquiry-based science, 14–16
Reading comprehension. *See* Text comprehension
Reading science. *See* Science reading
Reading strategies and text comprehension, 21
Reading strategy instruction, 49–50, 77
 anticipation guide, 81–83
 content teachers and, 98
 graphic organizer, 92–94
 KWL, 83–85
 principles and practice, 97–98
 prior knowledge monitoring and integration, 85–86
 Questioning the author (QTA), 88–90
 reciprocal teaching, 90–92
 sample lesson plans, 98–102
 SQ3R, 94–96
 text comprehension and, 78
 "Thick and Thin Questions" vignette, 79–80, 99–100
 think-pair-share, 86–88
 two-column note taking, 96–97, 101–102
Reciprocal teaching, 90–92
Refutational texts, 123
Report text, 106
Research report, 105
Revkin, A. K., 46
Rivard, R., 104
Robert F. Sibert Informational Book Award, 37
Robertson, A., 119
Robinson, P., 52
Role playing a trial, 41–42
Roots, 52, 54

School-based science writing genres, 105–109
School science radio show activity, 73
School science texts, 16
Schuder, T., 78

Schwartz, R., 58
Science author studies, 46–47
Science education, state of in American schools, 2
Science fair projects, 121–122
Science grammar, 49
 abstraction, 23–25
 density, 25–30
 impersonal authoritativeness, 31–32
 metaphorical realization of logical reasoning, 30–31
 technicality, 23
 school-based science genres, 105–109
Science journals, 115–116
Science literacy, 1, 14–16
Science reading:
 linguistic challenges, 22–32
 promoting success in, 51
 science education and, 14–16
 student experience with expository texts, 49–50
 See also Reading strategy instruction; Text comprehension
Science textbooks, 16, 35
Science trade books, 34–35
 advantages for using, 35–36
 author studies, 46–47
 biographical literature, 42–43
 empowering science learning, 41
 format of, 37–41
 illustrations in, 38, 39–40
 poetry studies, 43
 reading aloud, 44–45
 sources, 36–37, 44
 student reading skills and, 38–41
 study groups, 45–46
 unit study using, 41–42
Science vocabulary. *See* Vocabulary
Science writing. *See* Writing
Science writing genres, 105–109
Science writing heuristic, 124–125
Science writing-to-learn activities. *See* Writing-to-learn-science activities
Sciencing cycle, 9
Scientifically literate person, 4
Scientific inquiry, 2–3. *See also* Inquiry-based science
Scientist biographies, 42–43, 120–121
Sentence completion activity, 68–69
Sentence deconstruction and reintegration, 71–73
Silverstein, A. and V., 46
Simon, S., 46, 47
Situation model, 20

Skilled readers, 78
Sloan, C., 46
Small group activity, reciprocal
    teaching, 90–92
Source notes, 40–41
SQ3R, 94–96
Stafford, W., 43
Steele, P., 46
Stille, D. R., 46
Straits, W., 41, 45
Strategy instruction. *See* Reading
    strategy instruction
Straw, S., 104
Student achievement in science, 1
    inquiry-based science and, 5
Student attitudes toward science, 1–2
    inquiry-based science and, 4
Student experience with expository
    texts, 49–50
Study groups, 45–46
Subordinate clause, 26, 71–72, 129
Suffixes, 52, 54
Syntactic anatomy and integration,
    71–73

Table of contents, 39
Taxonomic report, 106
Taylor, J. A., 4
Teachers as raconteurs of science, 127
Teaching inquiry-based science, 8–9
Technicality, 23
Textbooks, 35
Text comprehension:
    abstraction, 23–25
    background knowledge, 21–22, 34
    density, 25–30
    impersonal authoritativeness, 31–32
    linguistic knowledge, 21–22
    metaphor, 30–31
    primary- and intermediate-grade
        texts, 19–22
    prior knowledge and, 81
    processes, 20–22
    reading strategies, 21
    reading strategy instruction and, 78
    situation model and cultural
        model, 20
    technicality, 23
"Thick and Thin Questions" vignette,
    79–80, 99–100
Thimmesh, C., 46
Think-pair-share, 86–88
Tivnan, T., 5
Topic, 112

Trade books. *See* Science trade books
Treagust, D., 50, 75–76
Turner, T., 127
Two-column note taking, 96–97,
    101–102

Unger, C., 44
Unit study, using informational books,
    41–42
Unsworth, L., 33
Urban, L., 30

van Meter, P., 78
Veel, R., 33, 76, 109
Verbs, 25
Visual display:
    graphic organizer, 92–94
    multimodal writing projects, 118–119
Vocabulary:
    concept definition word map,
        57–59, 113
    definition game, 66–68
    morphemic analysis, 52–56
    technical words and comprehension
        issues, 23
    think chart, 56–57
    vocabulary self collection (VSS),
        59–60
    word sort, 60–61

Washington Post/Children's Book
    Guild Nonfiction Award, 46
Watson, J., 71
Web logs, 117–118
Wellington, J., 15, 49, 78, 127
Wilson, C. D., 4
Word sort, 60–61
Writing, 103
    genre teaching cycle, 105–109
    importance in science, 103–104
    informal types, 111–112
    learning to write science, 104–111
    school-based science
        genres, 105–109
    types of for scientists, 105
    writing to learn science, 111–127
Writing-to-learn-science
    activities, 115
    analyzing analogies, 123–124
    biography book projects, 120–121
    class publications, 119–120
    concept mapping, 125
    cubing, 125–126
    e-pal projects, 122–123

journals, 115–116
learning logs, 116–117
multimodal writing projects, 118–119
Mystery Box Writing, 122
others, 126–127
Quickwrites, 126
refutational texts, 123
science fair projects, 121–122
science journals
science writing heuristic, 124–125
web logs, 117–118

Writing-to-learn-science instructional
   model
   dimensions of writing, 112
   implementation example, 113–115
   interactive-constructivist model,
      111–112
   positive environments, 112

Yore, L., 50, 75–76, 104, 125

Zales, C., 44

CORWIN
A SAGE Company

The Corwin logo—a raven striding across an open book—represents the union of courage and learning. Corwin is committed to improving education for all learners by publishing books and other professional development resources for those serving the field of PreK–12 education. By providing practical, hands-on materials, Corwin continues to carry out the promise of its motto: **"Helping Educators Do Their Work Better."**

National Science Teachers Association

The National Science Teachers Association is the largest professional organization in the world promoting excellence and innovation in science teaching and learning for all. NSTA's membership includes approximately 60,000 science teachers, science supervisors, administrators, scientists, business and industry representatives, and others involved in science education.

X